seeing
GOD

OTHER BOOKS BY DAVID ROPER:

A Burden Shared
Elijah: A Man Like Us
Growing Slowly Wise
In Quietness and Confidence
Jacob: The Fools God Chooses
A Man to Match the Mountain
Out of the Ordinary: God's Hand at Work in Everyday Lives
Psalm 23
Seasoned with Salt
Song of a Longing Heart
The Strength of a Man
Teach Us to Number Our Days

seeing GOD

MEET GOD IN THE UNEXPECTED

DAVID ROPER

DISCOVERY HOUSE
PUBLISHERS®

Discovery House Publishers is affiliated with RBC Ministries, Grand Rapids, Michigan.

Discovery House books are distributed to the trade exclusively by Barbour Publishing, Inc., Uhrichsville, Ohio.

Requests for permission to quote from this book should be directed to Permissions Department, Discovery House Publishers, P.O. Box 3566, Grand Rapids, MI 49501 or contact us by e-mail at permissionsdept@dhp.org.

All Scripture quotations, unless otherwise noted, are taken from the *Holy Bible, New International Version,*®. *NIV*®. Copyright © 1973, 1978, 1984 by Biblica, Inc.™ Used by permission of Zondervan. All rights reserved worldwide. www.zondervan.com

All italics in Scripture quotations indicate the author's emphasis.

Library of Congress Cataloging-in-Publication Data
Roper, David, 1933–
    Seeing God: meet God in the unexpected / David Roper.
      p. cm.
ISBN 978-1-57293-199-2
1. Christian life. I. Title
BV4501.3.R665   2006
248.4—dc22   2006006434
                                      CIP

Printed in the United States of America

11 12 13 14 / 8 7 6 5 4 3

Contents

Publisher's Foreword

Over the years, and through the publication of eleven books, David Roper has garnered a faithful following of readers. Men appreciate his spirit of the tough outdoorsman and his honest heart. Women resonate with his gentle spirit attuned to the whispers of the Holy Spirit. Strength in quiet confidence describes both David and his message.

Now, we are honored to provide this anthology of readings for those who already know and love David's writing, while at the same time introducing new readers to his works.

In *Seeing God* we have included excerpts from each of David Roper's eleven books, and the book titles are indicated at the end of each selection. Each selection or chapter (sixty in all) opens with a relevant Scripture.

The book is divided into three parts, based on the themes found in 2 Timothy 2:22, "Pursue righteousness, faith, love and peace, along with those who call on the Lord out of a pure heart," which reflect many of the major themes in David's writing.

Part 1, "Calling on the Lord," focuses on our relationship with God—its foundational aspects (Who are we? Who is God?) as well as its maintenance and renewal: communing with the Holy Spirit through prayer, Bible reading, and meditation on God's Word and message. Part 2, "Pursuing Righteousness and Faith," hones in on our daily walk with Christ, on issues of obedience and trust. Part 3, "Pursuing Love and Peace," challenges and encourages us in terms of our personal relationships—within our families and church communities and also with nonbelievers in the wider neighborhood.

We hope that you will enjoy having "the best of David Roper" in one volume and that it will also spur you on to read more of his books in their entirety.

PART 1

Calling on the Lord

We Share God's Glory

Then God said, "Let us make man in our image."
—Genesis 1:26

I must confess that I'm a humanist—like David, whose poem raises the best question of all: "What is man?" (Psalm 8:4).

What is man? Biologically he's a mammalian vertebrate; order: primate; genus: homo; species: sapiens. His body is made up of organs, tissues, cells, and protoplasm. Chemically he's composed mostly of water, a large quantity of carbon, and various amounts of iron, calcium, magnesium, phosphorus, sulfur, lime, nitrogen, and some mineral salts. Psychologically he has intellectual, emotional, and volitional powers and various instincts. He has on occasion dashed off a 4.2-second forty and leaped into the air a little over 7.5 feet.

But man has to be something more. We long for other, more complete explanations. Something in man refuses to be cribbed and confined and reaches out beyond mere scientific description. Eternity is in our hearts. We too ask, "What is man? What am I?"

Down inside us is a mystery from which comes our pursuit of excellence; our love of athletics, art, and music; our yearning to know and to be known; our deep discontent at our inability to live up to our own ideals. This is part of the "something more" that makes us truly human. That's why we want to know what it means to be a man.

We ask, as Saul Bellow did, "Is there nothing else between birth and death but what I can get out of this perversity—only a favorable balance of disorderly emotions? No freedom? Only impulses? And what about all the good I have in my heart—doesn't it mean anything? Is it simply a joke? A false hope that makes a man feel the illusion of worth?" Is this all there is?

And what about our instincts? We know that men were meant to be courageous, selfless, loyal. Manhood is deeply rooted and is a memory written in our hearts. We know the rules. We just can't comply. And in the end we get tired of trying to be a man. As G. K. Chesterton said, "Pessimism comes not when we get weary of doing evil but when we get weary of doing good." No, there must be something more.

What are we? The psalmist fills in the picture. God made man the summit of creation, the highest order of created beings, the most godlike creature in heaven and earth, only slightly less than God Himself. Man is the only creature who shares God's glory and honor. We have great dignity and worth. For all our foibles and flaws, we have vast potential for good in science and technology, in arts and letters. We have tremendous capacity to give and love, to know and to be known. No man has ever plumbed his own depths. We're wonderful because God made us so.

The poet's conclusion, therefore, is noteworthy:

> O Lord, our Lord,
>   how majestic is *your name* in all the earth! (Psalm 8:9).

His contemplation of man's greatness leads the poet to worship not man but the God who made man, who "crowned him with glory and honor" and "put everything under his feet" (Psalm 8:5–6).

And so we, along with the psalmist, give thanks to the One who made man—who formed the creative genius of Michelangelo, the music genius of Amadeus Mozart, the hand-eye coordination of Joe Montana. Contrary to our common belief, there are no self-made men. "It is he that hath made us, and not we ourselves" (Psalm 100:3 KJV). We know that it takes God to make men great, and we give thanks to Him for making us what we are. We must give credit where credit is due.

—The Strength of a Man

He Knew He Was Homesick

"For this son of mine was dead and is alive again; he was lost and is found." So they began to celebrate.
—Luke 15:24

A certain young man had a father who gave him a warm and safe home, food to eat, and most of all his love and loyalty. The young man could have lived happily ever after, but he didn't like the house rules. He wanted to be on his own.

The father thought otherwise; he knew a young man needed limits and respect for boundaries. His son would only be at odds with himself, utterly unhappy with a freedom that knew no fear, limits, or respect for others.

But the boy wanted to leap the fences. Life's mysteries beckoned; his pulse raced; he feared he might miss out on life. He must find himself; as we say, he had to have space.

His friends agreed. "It's good," they said, "for a man to assert himself. You have to risk the boy to find the man. There comes a time to be recognized, to get yourself free."

The boy demanded his inheritance. "After all, he argued, it's mine; I have it coming to me." So the father gave him his legacy. Now he could do as he pleased, never stopping to think that all he possessed came from his father. He wasn't thankful for his father's love.

He couldn't stay in his hometown—too many reminders of his father's presence—so, like Kipling, he looked for a place "where there ain't no Ten Commandments." He hied himself to San Francisco where a man can quickly find and lose himself. He bought a condo by the bay, a new wardrobe, an SUV. He was an instant sensation, one of the beautiful people.

He spent lavishly and threw himself into the company of trendy friends, but something was amiss. A persistent melancholy hounded him, a dreary sameness, a monotony that he could not shake. The unhappier he became, the more he diverted himself by celebrating. And then he realized his diversions controlled him. He could no longer be alone or free.

Most of his friends shared the same fate. They had that hollow look in their eyes; their faces told their story.

He went from bad to worse—a downturn that drove him to the sinks of skid row. He ran out of money and friends. Left with nothing but unsatisfied longing, he turned to drugs to ease the pain. He had neither morality nor modesty.

Then one day he awoke to remember his father's house and its joy. He remembered the good things: the love, the warmth, the knowledge that he belonged. He knew then he was homesick; he had to go home.

But not as a son. He had forfeited his right to be called his father's son. He would go and ask for a mere servant's role—anything to get back home. And so he packed a bag and caught a bus for home. On the way he rehearsed his lines: "Father, I have sinned against heaven and against you. I am no longer worthy to be called your son; make me like one of your hired men" (Luke 15:18–19).

When he was only a speck in the distance, his father saw him. He ran as fast as his faltering old legs could carry him, threw his arms around his son, and kissed him. He brought him to the house and gave him new clothes and shoes. Then he threw a barbecue for all the neighbors, and he told every guest, "This son of mine was dead, but now he's alive again."

Jesus told this story of the prodigal son more than two thousand years ago, but the picture of the waiting Father has not faded. Our heavenly Father still loves us and waits patiently and longingly for us to come home.

In one way or another, we are all like the wayward son. We have our dark ages. We fool around with sex, drugs, ambition, and a hundred other diversions. He permits us to use our bodies for self-gratification, our energy to pursue selfish ends, and even our minds to devise arguments against Him. And He will let us search restlessly, relentlessly, until we utterly weary ourselves. When we exhaust our options, we turn to Him. Before we can even ask for help, He wraps us in His arms and will not let us go.

—The Strength of a Man

God Has a Shepherd's Heart

The Lord is my shepherd, I shall not be in want.
—Psalm 23:1

The problem with most of us is that we have no clear picture of the God we long to worship. Our image of Him is clouded by the memory of cold cathedrals and bitter religions, by pastors or priests who put the fear of God into us, or by all that we suffered as children from fathers who were absent, emotionally detached, brutal, or weak. All of us have inexact notions of God.

Who is He? This is the question to which all others lead—the question that God Himself put into our hearts (and if He put it into our hearts, there must be an answer in His heart waiting to be revealed).

In Psalm 23:1 David gives us a comforting and compelling answer: "*Yahweh* is my shepherd." David used the name that God gave Himself. An older generation of scholars referred to the name as the "Ineffable Tetragrammaton"—the unutterable four-letter word. The Jews rarely pronounced the letters that make up God's name (written without vowels as YHWH) for fear of arousing God's wrath. Instead they substituted some lesser word like *Adonai* (my Lord) or *Elohim* (the generic name for God).

The term *Yahweh* comes from a form of the Hebrew verb "to be" and suggests a self-sufficient God. But that explanation is cold comfort to me. I prefer David's description: Yahweh is my *shepherd*.

Shepherd is a modest metaphor, yet one that is freighted with meaning. Part of the comparison is the portrayal of a shepherd and his sheep; the other is David's experience and ours. David paints a picture and puts us into it.

This is the genius of Psalm 23: It belongs to us; we can use David's words as our own.

David's opening statement, "The Lord is my shepherd," introduces the controlling image that appears throughout the poem. Each line elaborates the symbol, filling out the picture, showing us how our Shepherd-God leads us to that place where we shall no longer want.

David himself was a shepherd. He spent much of his youth tending his "few sheep in the desert" (1 Samuel 17:28). The desert is one of the best places in the world to learn. There are few distractions, and there is little that can be used. In such a place we're more inclined to think about the meaning of things rather than about what those things provide.

One day as David was watching his sheep, the idea came to him that God was like a shepherd. He thought of the incessant care that sheep require—their helplessness and defenselessness. He recalled their foolish straying from safe paths; their constant need for a guide. He thought of the time and patience it took for them to trust him before they would follow. He remembered the times when he led them through danger and they huddled close at his heels. He pondered the fact that he must think for his sheep, fight for them, guard them, and find their pasture and quiet pools. He remembered their bruises and scratches, which he bound up, and he marveled at how frequently he had to rescue them from harm. Yet not one of his sheep was aware of how well it was watched. Yes, he mused, God is very much like a good shepherd.

Ancient shepherds knew their sheep by name. They were acquainted with all their ways—their peculiarities, their characteristic marks, their tendencies, their idiosyncrasies.

Back then shepherds didn't drive their sheep; they led them. At the shepherd's morning call—a distinctive guttural sound—each flock would rise and follow its master to the feeding grounds. Even if two shepherds called their flocks at the same time and the sheep were intermingled, they never followed the wrong shepherd. All day long the sheep followed their own shepherd as he searched the wilderness looking for grassy meadows and sheltered pools where his flock could feed and drink in peace.

At certain times of the year it became necessary to move the flocks deeper into the wilderness, where predators lurked. But the sheep were always well guarded. Shepherds carried a "rod" (a heavy club) on their belts and a shepherd's staff in their hands. The staff had a crook that was used to extricate the sheep from perilous places or to restrain them from wandering away; the club was a weapon to ward off beasts.

Throughout the day each shepherd stayed close to his sheep, watching them carefully and protecting them from the slightest harm. When one sheep strayed, the shepherd searched for it until it was found. Then he laid it across his shoulders and brought it back home. At the end of the day, each shepherd led his flock to the safety of the fold and slept across the gate to protect his sheep.

A good shepherd *never* left his sheep alone. They would have been lost without him. His presence was their assurance.

Ezekiel announced the birth of the best of all shepherds long before He was born. He said that when He came, He would tend God's flock with tender, loving care.

Another Good Shepherd was on the way, one who would be one with the Father in pastoral compassion: "I will place over them one [unique] shepherd, my servant David, and he will tend them; he will tend them and be their shepherd. I the Lord will be their God, and my servant David will be a prince among them. I the Lord have spoken" (Ezekiel 34:23–24).

Another Good Shepherd: David's long-awaited Son, our Lord Jesus, that Great Shepherd who lays down His life for the sheep (John 10:11).

Some six hundred years later, Jesus stood near the place where David composed his Shepherd Song and said with quiet assurance,

> I [myself] am the good shepherd. The good shepherd lays down his life for the sheep. The hired hand is not the shepherd who owns the sheep. So when he sees the wolf coming, he abandons the sheep and runs away. Then the wolf attacks the flock and scatters it. The man runs away because he is a hired hand and cares nothing for the sheep.
>
> I am the good shepherd; I know my sheep and my sheep know me—just as the Father knows me and I know the Father—and I lay down my life for the sheep (John 10:11–15).

This is our Lord Jesus, "that great Shepherd of the sheep" (Hebrews 13:20).

He was one with the Father: He too saw us as "sheep without a shepherd." He "came to seek and to save what was lost" (Luke 19:10). He's the one who left the "ninety-nine on the hills" and went "to look for the one [sheep] that wandered away," forever establishing the value of one person and the Father's desire that not one of them should be lost (Matthew 18:12–14).

He has a shepherd's heart, beating with pure and generous love that counted not His own life-blood too dear a price to pay down as our ransom. He has a shepherd's eye that takes in the whole flock and misses not even the poor sheep wandering away on the mountains cold. He has a shepherd's faithfulness, which will never fail or forsake, leave us comfortless, nor flee when He sees the wolf coming. He has a shepherd's strength, so that He is well able to deliver us from the jaw of the lion or the paw of the bear. He has a shepherd's tenderness; no lamb so tiny that He will not carry it; no saint so weak that He will not gently lead; no soul so faint that He will not give it rest . . . His gentleness makes great (F. B. Meyer).

But there's more: The Good Shepherd laid down His life for the sheep. The Father issued the decree:

> Awake, O sword, against my shepherd,
>   against the man who is close to me! . . .
> Strike the shepherd . . . (Zechariah 13:7).

And the Shepherd was slain.

Since the beginning of time, religions have decreed that a lamb should give up its life for the shepherd. The shepherd would bring his lamb to the sanctuary, lean with all his weight on the lamb's head, and confess his sin. The lamb would be slain, and its blood would flow out—a life for a life.

What irony: Now the shepherd gives up His life for His lamb.

> He was pierced for *our* transgressions,
>   he was crushed for *our* iniquities;
> the punishment that brought us peace was upon him,
>   and by his wounds we are healed.
> We all, like sheep, have gone astray,
>   each of us has turned to his own way;
> and the Lord has laid on him the iniquity of us all (Isaiah 53:5–6).

The story is about the death of God. "He himself bore our sins in his body on the tree, so that we might die to sins and live for righteousness; by his wounds you have been healed" (1 Peter 2:24). He died for *all* sin—the obvious sins of murder, adultery, and theft as well as for the secret sins of selfishness and pride. He *Himself* bore our sins in His body on the cross. This was sin's final cure.

The normal way of looking at the Cross is to say that man was so bad and God was so mad that someone had to pay. But it was not anger that led Christ to be crucified; it was love. The Crucifixion is the point of the story: God loves us so much that He *Himself* took on our guilt. He internalized *all* our sin and healed it. When it was over He said, "It is finished!" There is nothing left for us to do but to enter into forgiving acceptance—and for those of us who have already entered it, to enter into more of it.

"But," you say, "why would He want me? He knows my sin, my wandering. I'm not good enough. I'm not sorry enough for my sin. I'm unable not to sin."

Our waywardness doesn't have to be explained to God. He's never surprised by anything we do. He sees everything at a single glance—what is, what could have been, what would have been apart from our sinful choices. He sees into the dark corners and crannies of our hearts and knows everything about us there is to know. But what He sees only draws out His love. There is no deeper motivation in God than love. It is His nature to love; He can do no other; "God is love" (1 John 4:8).

Do you have some nameless grief? Some vague, sad pain? Some inexplicable ache in your heart? Come to Him who made your heart. Jesus said, "Come to me, all you who are weary and burdened, and I will give you rest. Take my yoke upon you and learn from me, for I am gentle and humble in heart, and you will find rest for your souls. For my yoke is easy and my burden is light" (Matthew 11:28–30).

To know that God is like this, and to know this God, is rest. There is no more profound lesson than this: He is the one thing that we need.

Shepherd—the word carries with it thoughts of tenderness, security, and provision, yet it means nothing as long as I cannot say, "The Lord is *my* shepherd." What a difference that monosyllable makes—all the difference in the world. It means that I can have all of God's attention all of the time, just as though I'm the only one. I may be part of a flock, but I'm one of a kind.

It's one thing to say, "The Lord is a shepherd"; it's another to say, "The Lord is *my* shepherd." Martin Luther observed that faith is a matter of personal pronouns: *my* Lord and *my* God. This is the faith that saves.

Every morning the Shepherd "calls his own sheep by name and leads them out. When he has brought out all his own, he goes on ahead of them, and his sheep follow him because they know his voice" (John 10:3–4).

This morning as you awakened, His eyes swept over you; He called you by name and said, "Come, follow me." It's a once-for-all thing; it's an everyday thing.

> Come, let us bow down in worship,
>   let us kneel before the Lord our Maker;
> for he is our God
>   and we are the people of his pasture,
> the flock under his care .
>   —Psalm 95:6–7

—Psalm 23

God Longs to Save

"Neither do I condemn you . . .
Go now and leave your life of sin."
—John 8:11

When I was a much younger man, an older friend tried to dissuade me from an activity he considered sinful. "What would Jesus say if He returned and found you there?" he asked.

It's a good question—one worth asking from time to time. What if Jesus caught you smoking pot? What if He returned and found you at an X-rated movie? What if He found you in bed with another's wife? What would He say? Actually, we know what He would say if He caught us in sin. It happened once.

It was one of those days! Jesus was going about His business, trying to teach, when He was interrupted by shouts and sounds of scuffling. A group of clergymen barged in on His class and unceremoniously dumped a woman, disheveled and defiant, at His feet. They said dramatically, "Teacher, this woman was caught in the act of adultery. In the Law Moses commanded us to stone such women. Now what do you say" (John 8:4–5)?

Catapulting the woman into the crowd, the clergy shouted her sin for all to hear. Clearly they had no compassion for her; she was trash. Disdain for her flowed out of them like the tide. And just as certainly no passion for justice existed. Their motive was malice; they wanted to entrap Jesus. The woman was only bait.

They had a closed case. The Law was clear; adultery then was a capital offense (Leviticus 20:10; Deuteronomy 22:22). Their innuendo was plain. "*Moses* commanded us to stone such women. Now what do *you* say?" If Jesus took issue with Moses' Law, His critics could legitimately assail Him as a lawbreaker and discredit Him as a teacher. On the other hand, if He upheld the Law's judgment, He would no longer be the sinners' friend. They had Him either way! In chess you'd call their move a "fork."

Ignoring them, Jesus stooped over and started to write with His finger in the dirt. He must have been outraged at the way they unhallowed the woman. When they persisted in their questioning, He straightened up and said to them, "If any one of you is without sin, let him be the first to throw a stone at her" (John 8:7). Stooping down again, He wrote on the ground.

Her accusers slowly drifted away. The older ones first—they had the longest track record of sin—the others later, their silence and withdrawal a tacit admission of guilt. And Jesus was left alone with the woman. Looking up He said, "Dear lady, where are they? Has no one condemned you?" She replied calmly, respectfully, "No one, sir." And Jesus said, "Then neither do I condemn you. Go now and leave your life of sin" (see John 8:10–11).

Jesus didn't overlook her sin; He called her adultery sin. He knew the harm and heartbreak of it, and He upheld the Law. An adulterous lifestyle is what Jesus would call a "life of sin," and on another occasion He condemned even lustful thoughts. But God has no heart for throwing stones; judgment is His "alien" work (Isaiah 28:21). He longs rather to save, and Jesus is the incarnation of that longing.

The only sinless One, who could throw stones with impunity, did not do so because "God did not send his Son into the world to condemn the world, but to save [it]" (John 3:17). He paid the price for sin so justice could be satisfied and judgment averted. As Paul later wrote, "There is now no condemnation for those who are in Christ Jesus" (Romans 8:1).

This woman must have realized from the beginning that Jesus' sympathies were with her and against her accusers. Other men came to use her. This Man had come to save. And save her He did! Not merely from guilt but from sin's power! "Go now," He said, "and leave your life of sin." Her chains fell off; her heart was free.

This story of the fallen woman is what J. R. R. Tolkien would call a "eucatastrophe," where things come right after seeming to go irrevocably wrong. Villains are foiled, people in jeopardy are freed, justice is done, and the ending is happy.

—The Strength of a Man

The Lord Is Near

*When Jacob awoke from his sleep, he thought, "Surely the Lord is
in this place, and I was not aware of it."*
—Genesis 28:16

Jacob was on the run, fleeing from Esau's fury, lonely, desperate, and stripped of everything that gives meaning to human life, so lost that even God couldn't find him—or so he thought.

He came to "no particular place," as the Hebrew text suggests and, because night was falling, cleared a spot on the rubble-strewn ground, found a flat rock on which to rest his head, and lay down. In misery and exhaustion Jacob soon lapsed into a deep sleep in which he began to dream. In this dream God thrust into Jacob's life a revelation of His great love, a timely and necessary disclosure for the dejected fugitive.

In his dream Jacob envisioned a stairway, rising from the stone at his head, connecting heaven and earth. The traditional ladder is such a favorite image that it's a shame to give it up, yet it must be said that the picture of angels in their ungainly apparel scrambling up and down the rungs of a ladder leaves much to be desired. The term usually translated "ladder" actually suggests a stairway or stone ramp like those that led to the top of ziggurats, the terraced pyramids raised to worship the gods of that era.

The ziggurat with its steep stairway was essentially a symbol of man's efforts to plod his way up to God. One must trudge up a long, steep flight of stairs. It was hard work, but there was no other way to get help when you needed it (see Genesis 11:1–4).

It's odd how that pagan notion of scrabbling and clawing our way up to God has found its way into our own theology and thinking. Some early

Christian writers used the ladder as an analogy for spiritual progress, tracing the steps of Christian faith from one stage to another, rising higher by strong effort and good works, "grunting ourselves to God," as a friend of mine once put it. Walter Hilton's classic *The Ladder of Perfection* is based on that notion. The old camp-meeting song "We Are Climbing Jacob's Ladder" draws on the same association. In each case the emphasis is on the ascent of man.

What caught Jacob's attention, however, was not the stairway but the fact that God was standing *beside* or *alongside* him, for that's the meaning of the preposition translated "above" in Genesis 28:13. (The same Hebrew word is translated "nearby" in Genesis 18:2 and "before," in the sense of "in front of," in Genesis 45:1.) What is important to visualize is that God had come down the ramp. The God of Jacob's father, Isaac, and grandfather, Abraham, was at his side in this desolate place, contrary to Jacob's expectations and far from the traditional holy places he normally associated with God's presence.

"Surely the Lord is in *this place,* and I was not aware of it," Jacob declared with wide-eyed, childlike astonishment. "This [place] is none other than the house of God; this [stairway] is the gate of heaven" (Genesis 28:16–17).

Jacob got the message in the metaphor, but God was taking no chances. He highlighted the picture with a promise that would sustain Jacob through the weary days of character-building ahead: "*I am with you* and will watch over you wherever you go . . . *I will not leave you* until I have done what I have promised you" (Genesis 28:15).

This is our promise as well. "God has said, 'Never will I leave you; never will I forsake you' " (Hebrews 13:5). He is present with us whether we know it or not—in our joys but also in our sorrows; in our triumphs as well as in our confusion, disappointments, failures, frustrations, and bad judgments. While God is molding us, His love surrounds us—waiting, longing to make itself known.

God's presence is not a symbol, a manner of speaking, or a virtual reality, but the real thing—as real as it gets, as real as it was in the days of His incarnation. The difference is that now He is invisible to all but the eyes of faith.

In the upper room Jesus promised His disciples, "I will not leave you as orphans; *I will come to you.* Before long, the world will not see me anymore, but you will see me" (John 14:18–19).

Some say that Jesus was speaking of His second coming, but I rather think He was and is concerned with this present age in which He walks with us unseen. He is actually (not figuratively) with us, spiritually visible to those who love Him. "He who loves me will be loved by my Father," Jesus said, "and I too will love him and show myself to him" (John 14:21).

"Would not this be a good day for the Lord to come?" asks one of George MacDonald's characters. "Aye," replies his fellow traveler, "but is not this a good day for him to be walking beside us?" This rejoinder captures the essence of Jesus' promise.

Think, for example, of our Lord's post-resurrection appearance to the two disciples on the road to Emmaus. You know the story—how He fell in with them as they walked, expounding the Scriptures along the way. Then, when invited to eat with them, He "took bread, gave thanks, broke it, and began to give it to them" (Luke 24:30)—at which point, I suppose, they caught sight of the nail prints in His hands. "Then their eyes were opened and they recognized him, and he disappeared from their sight" (Luke 24:31). Or, as the text states literally, "He became invisible to them." He was *present* but unseen.

Or think of that day when He met again with His disciples in the upper room. He did not walk through the door or come in from the outside. He simply appeared, already with them in the room, present but unseen.

And so we, like Moses, endure, "because [we see] him who is invisible" (Hebrews 11:27). This is a perspective that requires a certain "obstinacy of belief," as C. S. Lewis would have it—a determination to believe against all odds and all evidence that our Lord is actually beside us every moment of every day. There is no moment when we are alone.

Our Lord Himself lived in continuous, conscious awareness of His Father's presence. "I am [never] alone," He said, "for my Father is with me" (John 16:32). That is the secret of His—and our—rich tranquillity.

When we know our Lord is present, we experience a delightful sense of peace no matter what our circumstances may be. A quiet serenity and security envelop us; foes, fears, afflictions, and doubts recede. We can forbear in any situation because we know "the Lord is near" (Philippians 4:5).

We, like Jacob, must practice God's presence, often pausing in the midst of our busy days to remind ourselves, "The Lord is here." We live surrounded by unseen realities, but our eyes are too often blind. Oh, that by humility and purity we might see Him who is invisible and see Him everywhere. "From youth we have only one vocation," says George MacDonald, "to grow eyes."

G. K. Chesterton was once asked by a reporter what he would say if Jesus were standing beside him. "He is," Chesterton replied with calm assurance.

—Jacob

Teach Us to Pray

*One day Jesus was praying in a certain place. When he finished,
one of his disciples said to him, "Lord, teach us to pray, just as
John taught his disciples."*
—Luke 11:1

Jesus baffles us as He baffled others. We see Him hard at work—confronting the powers of demons and men and defeating them, vindicating widows and orphans, directed by an unknown source of strength and wisdom. We watch and wonder. Where did He get His authority?

One of Jesus' disciples overheard Him pray and determined that Jesus' remarkable powers were related to prayer. Certainly this disciple, as everyone does, prayed now and then when the chips were down. Even the impious pray. But he wanted something more and so cried out, "Lord, teach us to pray!"

The Lord's Prayer follows, the prayer we've been taught to follow in form. But the Prayer is more than ritual; it's rather a revelation of the *meaning* of prayer. When Jesus called God *Father*, He was expressing utter dependence on Him.

Jesus followed no form in His prayers. On those occasions when we hear Him pray, such as in John 17, His prayers are informal. But if we listen, we will learn His secret—He prayed out of dependence. Perhaps the most startling of all Jesus' statements about Himself was His insistence that He too was a dependent being. Having laid aside the independent use of His deity, He declared, "By myself I can do nothing" (John 5:30).

And so He prayed without ceasing. Prayer was the environment in which He lived, the air He breathed. Subject to continual interruptions, busy beyond comparison, resisted by friends and foes, hassled and harried, He managed to keep in touch with God. Every situation was an occasion for prayer. When He held the small supply of bread and saw the multitude to be fed, He first gave thanks for God's supply. When He called Lazarus from the tomb, He first called on the Father. When the Greeks came seeking Him, knowing He had to come through, He asked God to glorify His name. Prayer was His principal work, and by this He carried on the rest.

His life was continuous prayer. No demands, only dependence; no clamoring for attention, only a quiet continual reliance on the Father who always heard Him (John 11:42).

Saints of the Middle Ages saw in *everything* a summons to prayer: a church bell, the flight of a swallow, a sunrise, the falling of a leaf. Our vision of ourselves as needy, dependent men makes life a matter of continuous prayer, so much a part of us that we can say with the psalmist, "I am a man of prayer" (Psalm 109:4).

And so the quintessence of life is prayer, not to demand but to wait with patience and submission, to long for and expect. By it everything else is done.

—*The Strength of a Man*

The Mystery of Prayer

Then the Lord said, "Shall I hide from Abraham what I am about to do? Abraham will surely become a great and powerful nation, and all nations on earth will be blessed through him. For I have chosen him, so that he will direct his children and his household after him to keep the way of the Lord by doing what is right and just, so that the Lord will bring about for Abraham what he has promised him."
—Genesis 18:17–19

I was raised in a religious tradition that prayed. We prayed before meals, before meetings, before bedtime, before football games, and before rodeos (to "that Big Cowboy in the sky").

I had no doubt that prayer did something; I just wasn't sure what it was, and, I must confess, even after all these years, I'm still a bit confused. I don't fully understand how prayer works.

Certainly when push comes to shove, we pray whether we understand prayer or not. It springs from us impulsively and instinctively in the face of necessity. There are no atheists in foxholes, as they say, nor in any other holes we dig for ourselves. When we're frightened out of our wits, when we're pushed beyond our limits, when we're pulled out of our comfort zones, we reflexively and involuntarily resort to prayer.

Yes, indeed. In *extremes,* we pray. "The natural thing is to go straight to the Father's knee," as George MacDonald said.

Yet the questions remain, or at least they do for me. How does prayer work? God is perfect wisdom. Does He need me to tell Him what to do? He is complete goodness. Does He need me to prod Him into doing the right thing? He is infinite wisdom. Does He need my counsel? Is it possible I can ask in such a way that God must change some vast eternal plan? Can I bend His ear and bend His will to mine? As Winnie the Pooh would say, "It's a puzzlement."

In the midst of all my uncertainty, however, one sure thing remains: Prayer changes *me*. It's one of the ways by which God turns me from the things that break my heart to the things that break His.

Take, for example, the story of Abraham and his intercession for the city of Sodom. It has particular value in understanding how prayer works, at least in terms of the way it works on me.

The story begins with God's verdict on Sodom: "How great is the out-cry against Sodom and Gomorrah and how very grave their sin!" (Genesis 18:20 NRSV). The Hebrew idiom underlying this statement can literally be rendered, "The sinners were in the Lord's face," suggesting a flagrant "in-your-face" attitude, a city raising its puny little fists in defiance of God.

For us Sodom was a sorry little city with no social value and worthy of nothing but immediate and catastrophic judgment, but for Abraham Sodom was flesh-and-blood people whom he knew and loved. Abraham had walked the streets of Sodom. He had talked with its citizens. He knew them by name. His nephew and family lived in the city. He had, on one occasion, delivered Sodom from a gang of thugs. It wasn't easy for him to give up Sodom, wicked though it was. Abraham grieved for its people.

God knew Abraham's aching heart and understood He must talk with His friend before He acted in judgment, so He and two of His angels clothed them-selves with flesh and came to visit Abraham under the Oaks of Mamre.

They came bearing a gift, as visitors sometimes do, the promise that Sarah would give birth to a long-awaited son. That business done, the Lord and His angels got up to leave, and Abraham, with the politeness of a good Semitic host, got up to go with them.

Abraham, the Lord, and the two angels trudged along for some distance in silence while the Lord communed with Himself.

Here in this soliloquy (Genesis 18:17–19) we see God's heart, His desire to let His dear friend Abraham in on His deepest secrets. "Is not this the time to take Abraham into my deepest counsel?" He says to Himself.

Was this disclosure necessary because Abraham was a superior being, more in touch with God than all the rest of us? No, indeed. God longs to re-veal His heart to everyone He loves: "Surely the Sovereign Lord does nothing without revealing his plan to his servants," the prophet said (Amos 3:7). He does so because that's what one does for a friend.

Friends open their hearts to one another; they hold nothing back. "I have called you friends," Jesus said to His disciples, "for *everything* that I learned from my Father I have made known to you" (John 15:15).

So when the angels turned away and went toward Sodom, "the Lord remained standing before Abraham." Unfortunately most versions render the text, "Abraham remained standing before the Lord" (Genesis 18:22), but that's a crashing mistake. The traditional Hebrew text states just the opposite. The original version tells us that God was actually standing before Abraham, patiently waiting for him to speak. As written, the text underscores God's passion to communicate with all of us. He, as in Abraham's day, stands continually before us, drawing us out, listening to our hearts, and waiting to reveal His own.

"Prayer is [God's] idea," Lloyd Ogilvie said. "[Our] desire to pray is the result of his greater desire to talk with us. *He* has something to say when we feel the urge to pray."

What follows, then, is the well-known account of that conversation between Abraham and God, or, if you please, that rap session in which Abraham pled Sodom's case, begging the Lord to spare Sodom for the sake of a few righteous souls and God agreeing to spare it for that number.

Abraham is faulted at times for his unwillingness to persist in his intercession, to wring Sodom's salvation from God for the sake of his nephew Lot (who, it appears, was the only good man in town). But, believe me, Abraham was never lacking in gumption and certainly not on this occasion. No, Abraham stopped praying because for the first time he saw the situation from God's point of view. At every step God's justice loomed larger; at every step more of God's justice entered into the man. In the end he was thinking more like God than ever before.

Here's the point: Abraham's prayer for Sodom didn't change anything—except Abraham. God had determined to judge that audacious sin-city because there was nothing in it worth saving. By prayer Abraham entered into God's wisdom, understood His thinking, and by it became a little more like God.

Prayer, then, whatever else it may be, is not calling God's attention to things He's not aware of, nor is it urging Him to do His duty. No, it's rather a conversation in which we speak our minds and God speaks His. We talk and we listen until we get into His mind and He gets into ours.

All of which means that when we get down to praying, we don't have to worry about what to say or how to say it. We can say whatever is in us. Though our prayers may spring from anxious fear or angry, ungodly thoughts of personal revenge, God will take those prayers into His heart and turn them into something else, and in the process He will turn us into something else.

I think that's what Paul meant when he wrote: "Do not be anxious about anything, but in everything, by prayer and petition, with thanksgiving, present your requests to God. And the peace of God, which transcends all understanding, will guard your hearts and your minds in Christ Jesus" (Philippians 4:6–7).

There's no promise here that anything or anyone is changed by our prayers except our state of mind. God's tranquillity takes the place of our anxiety; His peace transcends our panic. Prayer, thus wrung out of us by our deepest needs, has been turned into something yet more profound. In our praying *we* have been transformed.

This is God at work. This is the business of prayer.

—In Quietness and Confidence

Praying for a Cure

Is any one of you in trouble? He should pray. Is anyone happy?
Let him sing songs of praise. Is any one of you sick? He should
call the elders of the church to pray over him and anoint him with
oil in the name of the Lord. And the prayer offered in faith will
make the sick person well; the Lord will raise him up. If he has
sinned, he will be forgiven. Therefore confess your sins to each
other and pray for each other so that you may be healed. The
prayer of a righteous man is powerful and effective.
—James 5:13–16

It's incongruous that James would conclude his book with instructions on healing the body when his preoccupation throughout has been with the health and welfare of our souls. Though I do believe God heals, I assume He's concerned in this text not with physical illness but with the *soul*-sickness that so frequently attends our pilgrimage. Let me explain.

The word *sick* in verse 13 actually means "helpless" or "impotent," and though it's often used in the Gospels and Acts to refer to physical weakness, in the Epistles it almost always refers to *spiritual* limitation and disability. The context of James suggests the latter meaning.

The word *sick* appears again in verse 15. Here a different Greek word occurs that suggests weariness and fatigue. It's found in only one other place in the New Testament: "Consider him who endured such opposition from sinful men, so that you will not *grow weary* and lose heart" (Hebrews 12:3–4).

I understand James's text, then, as a word of encouragement to those who have been decimated by sin—who have tasted habitual defeat and have become discouraged in their struggle against besetting sins. He's concerned with the deep, penetrating pain that overwhelms us when we find ourselves in the grip of sinful habits, passions, and obsessive behaviors from which we find it difficult, if not impossible, to escape. We're beat; we're sunk; we've had it.

James assures us that we need not soldier on alone. We can call for the elders—mature fellow travelers—and ask for their prayers. Their intercessions, James assures us, will rekindle our weary spirits and renew our desire to press on. God Himself, who refreshes us with His forgiving presence, will "raise [us] up" from despair and gloom, and thus "the prayer of faith" will bring about our healing. There will be an end to sin's domination.

The "anointing"? Just a gentle reminder that our Lord Jesus, the Spirit of Holiness (whose presence is aptly symbolized by medicinal oil), is the One who heals us and makes us holy. There is a balm in Gilead to heal the sin-sick soul.

Some sins are too much for us. We cannot deal with them alone but need the efforts of other, more mature believers to help us gain release from Satan who has taken us captive to do his will. To struggle alone is to wither and die.

Martin Luther wrote, "No man should be alone when he opposes Satan. The church was instituted for this purpose, that hands may be joined together and one may help another. If the prayer of one doesn't help, the prayer of another will."

"Therefore," James concludes, "confess your sins to *each other* and pray for *each other* so that you may be healed. The prayer of a righteous man is powerful and effective."

It seems odd that James would move from calling for the elders to calling for grass-roots help, but I believe he's thinking here of *preventative* maintenance. We don't have to wait until evil overwhelms us and extreme measures become necessary. We can get help right now.

We can find a soul mate, a trusted ally who will stand with us in our battle against sin, a kind and gentle friend who will listen to our deepest motivations, jealousies, frustrations, and inclinations without judgment and censure, a caring presence, a loyal confidant to whom we can say without reservation, "This is the truth about me." Someone who will gently ask us about our secret thoughts, our darkest passions, our unobserved and unguarded moments—and then ask us if we have lied.

"Two are better than one," said the philosopher,

because they have a good return for their work:
If one falls down,
    his friend can help him up.
But pity the man who falls
    and has no one to help him up! (Ecclesiastes 4:9–10).

As Dietrich Bonhoeffer said, "Confession is not a divine law, but an offer of divine help for the sinner."

Prayer is a primary factor in this fellowship. We cannot fix others; we cannot change them; we cannot really help them. We can only take them to our Great High Priest, who alone gives "help [in] time of need" (Hebrews 4:16).

Prayer, in the sense that it brings us to God, is "powerful and effective." It is therapeutic; it heals! It is as God has promised—not that He will put an end to every physical affliction but that He will put an end to sin. This He will do in His good time and as surely as His own good name.

It seems a small thing merely to pray. Isn't there something else we must do? Indeed, but nothing essential. Prayer is the thing we must do before anything else is done. Remember Jesus' words to Simon Peter, "Satan has asked to sift you as wheat. *But I have prayed for you*" (Luke 22:31–32).

If we pray for sin's cure, something beyond us will be done: Sinners will begin to "be healed," says James, using a verb tense that suggests a *state* of healing. God will flow through our prayers to beget spiritual health and wholeness.

—Growing Slowly Wise

Crying Out of the Depths

*O God of my father Abraham, God of my father Isaac, O Lord,
who said to me, "Go back to your country and your relatives, and
I will make you prosper," I am unworthy of all the kindness and
faithfulness you have shown your servant. I had only my staff
when I crossed this Jordan, but now I have become two groups.
Save me, I pray, from the hand of my brother Esau, for I am
afraid he will come and attack me, and also the mothers with their
children. But you have said, "I will surely make you prosper and
will make your descendants like the sand of the sea, which cannot
be counted."*
—Genesis 32:9–12

We pray best when we have nothing going for us. "The best disposition for praying," said Augustine, "is that of being desolate, forsaken, stripped of everything."

Consider Jacob. When messengers announced Esau's advance, Jacob, filled with fear, began to pray. He began and ended his plea by reminding God of His promise: "You said!" (Genesis 32:9, 12).

"Ah, He had God in his power then," F. B. Meyer reflects. "God puts Himself within our reach in His promises . . . He cannot say nay—He must do as He has said."

God had promised to be with Jacob and bring him back to the land (Genesis 28:13–15). Thus Jacob could appeal to God's word. The Lord had promised to protect him, and He is the only One who cannot lie (Titus 1:2 NASB).

God is true. What He has promised He will do. We can rest in the integrity of His word. But we must be sure that we stand on God's actual word when we claim a promise, for then and only then do we have the assurance that God will come through. He is bound to do only what He has said He will do—nothing more or less.

Naïve, uninformed faith can be dangerous. I have a friend whose older brother once assured her that an umbrella had enough lift to hold her up if she would only "believe." So "by faith" she jumped off a barn roof, fell twenty feet straight down, and knocked herself out. And then, because she believed that the problem was a failure of faith, she tried again with precisely the same result. She got the message the second time around!

Faith must be informed—grounded on a clear understanding of what God has actually said. Faith has no power in itself. It counts only when it is based on a plain and unambiguous promise from God. Anything else is wishful thinking.

Case in point: God has promised, "Ask whatever you wish, and it will be given you. This is to my Father's glory, *that you bear much fruit*" (John 15:7–8).

This is not an unequivocal promise that God will respond affirmatively to every prayer we utter but rather a promise that He will grant every longing of ours for the fruit of the Spirit—love, joy, peace, patience, kindness, goodness, faithfulness, gentleness, and self-control. If we hunger and thirst for holiness and ask Him for it, He will begin to satisfy us. That's a promise we can count on, and "God don't make promises He don't keep," as Bob Dylan once pointed out.

Next Jacob moved to confession: "I am unworthy of the least of your love," he prayed, using a word for "least" that suggests the tiniest object. "Deliver me!" (see Genesis 32:10–11).

What an odd juxtaposition: "I am unworthy of salvation . . . Save me!"

Unlike those who have it all together, Jacob realized that anything he brought to God had already been ruined by sin. He saw himself as the man least worthy of God's grace. Yet he could pray for mercy, for his hope lay not in his own worth but in the promise of God to look with favor on those who throw themselves in penitence at His feet. Humility and contrition are the keys that open the heart of God.

Authentic prayer is a crying out of the depths (Psalm 130:1). It wells up from the soul that acknowledges its own deep depravity. Such prayers are offered by those who are thoroughly convicted of their sin and shame but at the same time convinced of God's grace that flows forth to undeserving sinners.

God hears best those who cry out like the tax collector in Jesus' parable, "Be merciful to me, *the* sinner!" (Luke 18:13 NASB).

Yet isn't it odd? Jacob had scarcely finished his prayer of contrition and trust when he resorted to his earlier tactic, relying again on his own ingenious scheme for self-preservation (Genesis 32:7–8, 13–21). It would have been better for Jacob to wait for God to show him *His* plan. This would have led him in ways he could never have imagined.

Not so odd, however, as I think about it. Jacob is just like me.

—Jacob

Bringing Every Need to God

*The wife of a man from the company of the prophets
cried out to Elisha, "Your servant my husband is dead, and you
know that he revered the Lord. But now his creditor is coming to
take my two boys as his slaves."
Elisha replied to her, "How can I help you? Tell me, what do you
have in your house?"*
—2 Kings 4:1–2

This woman's story is one of accumulated grief: Her husband died and left her destitute and deeply in debt; then her creditors came knocking at her door, demanding that she pay up or sell her two sons into slavery to compensate them.

Immediately and with sound wisdom she went to Elisha, the embodiment of God's presence in the land. Her words are a reminder that even those who "fear the Lord" may find themselves in deep trouble.

When Elisha heard the woman's plea, he didn't rush to meet her need as we're inclined to do. Had he done so, she might have gained a little comfort, but not from the highest source, and she would have gained it too soon for her own good. No, instead Elisha asked the woman what she had at hand. "Nothing," she said, "except a little oil."

His response? "Go around and ask all your neighbors for empty jars. Don't ask for just a few. Then go inside and shut the door behind you and your sons. Pour oil into all the jars, and as each is filled, put it to one side" (4:4).

When I first read the prophet's words, I thought of Jesus' words, "When you pray, go into your room [in the interior of the house], *close the door* and pray to your Father, who is unseen. Then your Father, who sees what is done in secret, will reward you" (Matthew 6:6). Nothing is said about prayer in the Old Testament account, but it's significant to me that Jesus' phrase, translated "close the door," corresponds roughly to the Greek translation of this Old Testament text, which Jesus Himself read and frequently quoted.[1] Could it be that He had this story in mind?

If so, I suggest that prayer is a matter of shutting ourselves away from all other dependencies—from background, experience, training, and past accomplishments, from all the props of reason and intellect, closing everything and everyone out, and closeting ourselves with God alone (see also 2 Kings 4:33). We detach ourselves from all outward things and attach ourselves inwardly to the Lord alone. This is where God works His wonders.

So, as the story goes, Elisha directed the widow to "shut the door behind her and her sons. They brought the jars to her and she kept pouring. When all the jars were full, she said to her son, 'Bring me another one.'

"But he replied, 'There is not a jar left.' Then the oil stopped flowing" (4:5–6). Then the widow sold the oil, paid off her debts, and lived on what remained.

The widow's needs were met, but something more important occurred: She learned to carry *everything* to God in prayer, or so I believe.

It seems that the early church asked its senior members to take on a particular ministry of love and prayer. This has now become my special work. I grieve with a friend over a prodigal son and can think of nothing hopeful to say. And so I pray. I listen to a pastor whose heart is broken by criticism and disapproval, and I can do nothing to change others' perceptions of him and his ministry. And so I pray. I stand by the bed of a desperately ill child, and I have no power to heal. And so I pray.

I pray, but more important, by my praying I teach *others* to pray. I may not be able to bring help to those in deep and desperate need, but I can encourage them to bring every need to the One who gives "grace to help us in our time of need" (Hebrews 4:16). This is my deepest joy. Elisha could have met this woman's dearth by giving her a gift of money or gathering food from her friends, but he gave her a greater gift—the gift of a lifetime: He taught *her* to pray.

—Seasoned with Salt

---

1. The only difference is that the Greek translation of 2 Kings 4:4 uses an intensified form of the verb and puts it in the future tense: *apokleiseis tân thuran* (You shall shut the door *tight!*). Jesus uses the simple form of the same verb and states the action as participle, *kleisas tân thuran* (having shut the door).

Grazing on God

He makes me lie down in green pastures,
he leads me beside quiet waters.
—Psalm 23:2

Left to ourselves we would have nothing more than restlessness, driven by the realization that there is something more to know and love. But God will not leave us to ourselves. He *makes* us lie down in green pastures. He *leads* us by quiet waters.

The verbs suggest gentle persuasion—a shepherd patiently, persistently encouraging his sheep to the place where their hungers and thirsts will be assuaged.

In David's day "green pastures" were oases, verdant places in the desert toward which shepherds led their thirsty flocks. Left to themselves sheep would wander off into the wilderness and die. Experienced shepherds knew the terrain and urged their flocks toward familiar grasslands and streams where they could forage and feed, lie down and rest.

The picture here is not of sheep grazing and drinking, but at rest, lying down—"stretched out" to use David's word. The verb *leads* suggests a slow and leisurely pace. The scene is one of tranquillity, satisfaction, and rest.

The common practice of shepherds was to graze their flocks in rough pasture early in the morning, leading them to better grasses as the morning progressed, and then coming to a cool and shaded oasis for noontime rest.

The image of placid waters emphasizes the concept of rest—the condition of having all our passions satisfied. Augustine cried out, "What will *make* me take my rest in You . . . so I can forget my restlessness and take hold of You, the one good thing in my life?"

The compulsion begins with God. God makes the first move; He takes the initiative—calling us, leading us to a place of rest.

It's not that we're seeking God; He is seeking us. "There is a property in God of thirst and longing," said Dame Julian of Norwich. "He hath longing to have us."

God's cry to wayward Adam and Eve, "Where are you?" (Genesis 3:9), suggests the loneliness He feels when separated from those He loves. G. K. Chesterton suggested that the whole Bible is about the "loneliness of God." I like the thought that in some inexplicable way God misses me; that He can't bear to be separated from me; that I'm always on His mind; that He patiently, insistently calls me, seeks me, not for my own sake alone, but for His. He cries, "Where are you?"

Deep within us is a place for God. We were made for God, and without His love we ache in loneliness and emptiness. He calls from deep space to our depths: "deep calls to deep" (Psalm 42:7).

David put it this way,

> My heart says of you, "Seek his face!"
> Your face, Lord, I will seek (Psalm 27:8).

God spoke to the depths of David's heart, uttering His heart's desire: "Seek My face." And David responded with alacrity, "I will seek Your face, Lord."

And so it is: God calls us—seeking us to seek Him—and our hearts resonate with longing for Him.

That understanding has radically changed the way I look at my relationship to God: It is now neither duty nor discipline—a regimen I impose on myself like a hundred sit-ups and fifty push-ups each day—but a response, an answer, to One who has been calling me all my life.

But what are those green pastures and quiet waters to which He leads us? And where are they? What is the reality behind these metaphors?

The real thing is God Himself. *He* is our "true pasture" (Jeremiah 50:7) and our pool of quiet water. He is our true nourishment, our living water. If we do not take Him in, we will starve.

There is a hunger in the human heart that nothing but God can satisfy. There is a thirst that no one but He can quench. "I am the bread of life. He who comes to me will *never* go hungry, and he who believes in me will *never* be thirsty" (John 6:35).

But how do we graze on God? How do we drink Him in?

The process begins, as all relationships do, with a "meeting." As David said:

> As the deer pants for streams of water,
>   so my soul pants for you, O God.
> My soul thirsts . . . for the living God.
>   When can I go and meet with God? (Psalm 42:1–2).

God is a real person. He is not a human invention, a concept, a theory, or a projection of ourselves. He is overwhelmingly alive—real beyond our wildest dreams. He can be "met" to use David's commonplace word.

A. W. Tozer wrote, "God is a Person and as such can be cultivated as any person can. God is a Person and in the depths of his mighty nature he thinks, wills, enjoys, feels, loves, desires and suffers as any other person may. God is a Person and can be known in increasing degrees of intimacy as we prepare our hearts for the wonder of it."

There's the reality, but there's also the rub: Are we willing to prepare ourselves to meet Him? He responds to the slightest approach, but we're only as close as we want to be. "If . . . you seek the Lord your God, you will find him," Moses promised, then added this proviso: "if you look for him with all your heart and with all your soul" (Deuteronomy 4:29).

We don't have to look very hard or very long for God. He's only as far away as our hearts (Romans 10:8–9), but He will not intrude. He calls us but then waits for our answer. Our progress toward Him is determined by our desire to engage Him in a personal way—to *know* Him.

We say, "Something's wrong with me; I'm not happy; there must be something more," but we do nothing about our discontent. It's this mood of resignation that keeps us from joy. Our first task is to get honest with ourselves. Do we want God or not? If we do, we must be willing to make the effort to respond to Him. "Come near to God," says James 4:8, "and he will come near to you." It's a matter of desire. "O God, you are my God, *earnestly* I seek you" (Psalm 63:1).

Henri Nouwen said, "If we really believe not only that God exists, but that he is actively present in our lives—healing, teaching, and guiding—we need to set aside a time and space to give him our undivided attention." Where can we find a quiet place in the midst of the din and demands of this world? "In a crowd it's difficult to see God," Augustine said. "This vision craves secret retirement."

There is a meeting place—a time and place where we can meet with God and hear His thoughts and He can hear ours; a time for the two of us where He can have our full attention and we can have His.

Solitude is where we are least alone and where our deepest loneliness can be relieved. It's a healing place where God can repair the damage done by the noise and pressure of the world. "The more you visit it," Thomas à Kempis said, "the more you will want to return."

The first step is to find a Bible, a quiet place, and an uninterrupted period of time. Sit quietly and remind yourself that you're in the presence of God. He is there with you, eager to meet with you. "Stay in that secret place," A. W. Tozer said, "till the surrounding noises begin to fade out of your heart, till a sense of God's presence has enveloped you. Listen for His inward voice till you learn to recognize it."

Until we take time to be quiet, we'll not hear God. God cannot be heard in noise and restlessness. Only in silence. He will speak to us if we will give Him a chance, if we will listen, if we will be quiet. "Be still," the psalmist sang, "and know that I am God" (Psalm 46:10).

"Listen, listen to me," God pleads,

> and eat what is good,
>> and your soul will delight in the richest of fare.
> Give ear and come to me;
>> hear me, that your soul may live (Isaiah 55:2–3).

Listen to Him. There's no other way to take Him in. "When your words came, I *ate* them," says Jeremiah 15:16. Sit at His feet and let Him feed you. That's the "better" place to be (Luke 10:38–42).

Jesus said to the best-read Bible students of His day, "You diligently study the Scriptures because you think that by them you possess eternal life. These are the Scriptures that testify about me" (John 5:39).

The scholars read the Bible, but they didn't listen to God; they never heard His voice. We should do more than read words; we should seek "the Word exposed in the words," as Karl Barth said. We want to move beyond information to seeing God and being informed and shaped by His truth. There's a passing exhilaration—the joy of discovery—in acquiring knowledge about the Bible, but there's no life in it. The Bible is not an end in itself but a stimulus to our interaction with God.

Start with a conscious desire to engage Him in a personal way. Select a portion of Scripture—a verse, a paragraph, a chapter—and read it over and over. Think of Him as present and speaking to you, disclosing His mind and emotions and will. God is articulate: He speaks to us through His Word. Meditate on His words until His thoughts begin to take shape in your mind.

Thoughts is exactly the right word, because that's precisely what the Bible is—the *mind* of the Lord (1 Corinthians 2:6–16). When we read His Word, we are reading His mind—what He knows, what He feels, what He wants, what He enjoys, what He desires, what He loves, what He hates.

Take time to reflect on what He is saying. Think about each word. Give yourself time for prayerful contemplation until God's heart is revealed and your heart is exposed. As Jean-Pierre de Caussade advised, "Read quietly, slowly, word for word to enter into the subject more with the heart than with the mind. From time to time make short pauses to allow these truths time to flow through all the recesses of the soul."

Listen carefully to the words that touch your emotions and meditate on His goodness. Feed on His faithfulness. Think about His kindness and those glimpses of His unfailing love that motivate you to love Him more (Psalm 48:9). Savor His words. *"Taste* and see that the Lord is good" (Psalm 34:8).

Mother Teresa told Henri Nouwen to "spend one hour a day in adoration of the Lord and you'll be all right." Mother Teresa might say something different to you and me. So much depends on our temperament, our family and job demands, the state of our health, our age and level of maturity. At first ten or fifteen minutes may be all we can manage. Then perhaps we will be ready for an hour every day. It's not important how much time we spend at first. The important thing is to make a beginning. God's Spirit will let us know where to go from there.

Our reading should be toward relishing God, delighting in Him, gazing at His beauty, as David said (Psalm 27:4). When we approach God in that way, it inclines us to want more of Him. "I have tasted Thee," Augustine said, "and now I hunger for Thee."

There's no need to worry about texts that we don't understand. Some meanings will escape us. Everything difficult indicates something more than our hearts can yet embrace. As Jesus said to His disciples, "I have much more to say to you, more than you can now bear" (John 16:12). There's much that we will never know, but some of the hard questions will be answered when we're ready for them.

God can never be understood through the intellect. Insight arises from purity of heart—from love, humility, and a desire to obey. It's the pure in heart who see God, Jesus said (Matthew 5:8). The more of God's truth we know and want to obey, the more we know. As George MacDonald said, "The words of the Lord are seeds sown in our hearts by the sower. They have to fall into our hearts to grow. Meditation and prayer must water them and obedience keep them in the light. Thus they will bear fruit for the Lord's gathering."

Nor should we worry about our doubts. How could God possibly reveal Himself in a way that would leave no room for doubt?

Madeleine L'Engle said, "Those who believe they believe in God . . . without anguish of mind, without uncertainty, without doubt, and even at times without despair, believe only in the idea of God, and not in God himself."

Uncertainty is the name of the game. The best thing is to take our questionings and doubts directly to God, as David often did. His psalms are filled with discomfort and disagreement with God's ways. He fills page after page with confusion and disbelief. It's good to do so. God can handle our hesitancy.

Sometimes we're mentally dull or emotionally flat, weary, and tired. On such occasions it's worthless to try to make ourselves think more deeply or respond more intensely. If the value of our times alone with God depends on our emotional state, we will always be troubled. We should never worry about how we feel. Even when our minds are confused or our hearts are cold, we can learn from our solitude. Don't try to make your heart love God. Just give it to Him.

If we're having a hard time with God, if we don't yet trust His heart, we should read the Gospels—Matthew, Mark, Luke, and John. There we hear what Jesus said and did and what was said about Him. There we see Him making visible the invisible God. When Philip, Jesus' disciple, asked to see God, Jesus replied, "Don't you know me, Philip, even after I have been among you such a long time? Anyone who has seen me has seen the Father. How can you say, 'Show us the Father'?" (John 14:9).

The main use of the Gospels is to help us see the character of God made real, personal, and understandable in Jesus. What we see Jesus doing—caring, suffering, weeping, calling, seeking—is what God is doing and has been doing all along. If you can't love God, try to see Him in Jesus. There He's revealed as One who has no limits to His love; One to whom we can come with all our doubts, disappointments, and misjudgments; One "whom we can approach without fear and to whom we can submit ourselves without despair," as Blaise Pascal said. In the Gospels we see that God is the only God worth having.

As we listen to God, we should answer. This is prayer—our response to the revelation and unfolding of God's heart. "My God, Thy creature answers Thee," said the French poet Mussett. Prayer, understood in that way, is an extension of our visits with God rather than something tacked on.

Our meetings with God are like a polite conversation with a friend. They're not monologues in which one person does all the talking but dialogues in which we listen thoughtfully to one another's self-disclosure and then respond.

One of my colleagues describes the process this way: If we're reading a note from a loved one in which we're praised, loved, appreciated, counseled, corrected, and helped in various ways and that individual is present in the room while we read, it's only right that we should express thanks, reciprocate love, ask questions, and in other ways react to the message. It would be rude to do otherwise. This is prayer.

Around 1370 a book was published with the title *The Cloud of Unknowing.* It's thought that the author was a spiritual director in a monastery, but we don't know his name. Much of what he wrote is hard to understand, but when it comes to prayer he was profoundly simple. God, he said, can be known even through "the cloud of unknowing" by responding to Him with "just a little word . . . the shorter it is the better."

If you don't know where to start, pray David's psalms. David's life was characterized by prayer—"I am a man of prayer," he said (Psalm 109:4). The translators supply "a man of," but the text reads simply, "I am prayer." Prayer was the essence of David's life and his genius, as it is ours. We have this access to God; this intimacy with Him; this opportunity to receive all that the heart of God has stored up for us. It is the means by which we receive God's gifts; the means by which everything is done. David teaches us to pray.

Prayer is worship. Our praying should be full of adoration, affection, and fondness for God—that He is who He is; that He created us in order to have someone on whom He could shower His love; that He stretched out His arms on the cross; that He intends, in the fullest sense, to make whole men and women out of us. In worship, as the old word *worth-ship* implies, we declare what we value the most. It is one of the best ways in the world to love God.

Prayer is the highest expression of our dependence on God. It is asking for what we want. We can ask for anything—even the most difficult things. "Do not be anxious about anything, but in everything, by prayer and petition, with thanksgiving, present your requests to God" (Philippians 4:6). Anything large enough to occupy our minds is large enough to hang a prayer on.

Prayer, however, by its nature is *requesting.* It is not insisting or clamoring. We can make no demands of God or deals with Him. Furthermore, we're coming to a friend. Friends don't make demands. They ask and then wait. We wait with patience and submission until God gives us what we request— or something more.

Prayer is asking for understanding. It is the means by which we comprehend what God is saying to us in His Word. The process by which we gain awareness of His mind is not natural, but supernatural: spiritual things are discerned spiritually (1 Corinthians 2:6–16). There is truth that can never be grasped by the human intellect. It cannot be discovered; it must be disclosed. Certainly we can understand the facts in the Bible apart from God's help, but we can never plumb its depths, never fully appreciate "what God has prepared for those who love him" (1 Corinthians 2:9). We must pray and wait for truth to come honestly into our minds.

Prayer moves what we know from our heads to our hearts; it's our hedge against hypocrisy, the way by which we begin to ring true. Our perceptions of truth are always ahead of our condition. Prayer brings us more into conformity; it bridges the gap between what we know and what we are.

Prayer focuses and unites our fragmented hearts. We have a thousand necessities. It's impossible for us to purify them and simplify them and integrate them into one. David prayed: "Give me an undivided heart" (Psalm 86:11). He wanted to love God with his whole soul, but he couldn't sustain the effort. Other interests and affections pulled him and divided him, so he asked God to guard his heart and unite its affections into one.

Psalm 90:14 says,

> Satisfy us in the morning with your unfailing love,
> that we may sing for joy and be glad all our days.

Centering on God has to be done each morning as though it had never been done before. In that quiet place He comforts us, He instructs us, He listens to us, He prepares our hearts and strengthens us for the day. There we learn to love Him and worship Him again; we esteem His words and defer to Him once more; we get His fresh perspective on the problems and possibilities of our day.

Then we should take His presence with us all through the day—journey-ing, pausing, waiting, listening, recalling what He said to us in the morning. He is our teacher, our philosopher, our friend; our gentlest, kindest, most interesting companion.

In God's presence there is satisfaction: His lush meadows are boundless; His still water runs deep. "There," I say to myself "[I] will lie down in good grazing land, and there [I] will feed in a rich pasture" (Ezekiel 34:14).

—Psalm 23

Reading and Heeding God's Word

For there is nothing hidden that will not be disclosed, and nothing
concealed that will not be known or brought out into the open.
Therefore consider carefully how you listen. Whoever has will be
given more; whoever does not have, even what he thinks he has will
be taken from him.
—Luke 8:17–18

There are two groups envisioned here: the "haves" and "have-nots." The "haves" are those who have soft and submissive hearts. They will be given more knowledge. The "have-nots" are those who have hardened their hearts. What knowledge they once had is taken away. The truth fades into forgetfulness.

If we do not want God, He will not foist Himself on us. To do so would trivialize His Word and brutalize us. Unlived truth hardens the heart and breeds contempt. For us to know more when we will not live it is our worst judgment.

So God in His love takes His Word away; He sends a famine—"not a famine of food . . . but a famine of hearing the words of the Lord" (Amos 8:11). We read the Bible, but we get nothing from it. We study it, but we go away empty-handed and confused.

George MacDonald wrote: "What [the biblical writers] care about is plain enough to the true heart, however it is far from plain to the man whose desire to understand goes ahead of his obedience . . . He who does that which he sees, shall understand; he who is set upon understanding rather than doing, shall go on stumbling and mistaking and speaking foolishness."

These days so many approach the Word purely as an object of intellectual pursuit, as though truth can be known by the mind alone. But the more we pursue God in this way, the more distant He becomes. Then terrible things begin to happen to us: Knowledge takes the place of wisdom; hubris takes the place of humility. The process breaks down into positions, disagreements, and intellectual pride.

Truth cannot be known through the intellect; it must be known through the heart. The more we love God and obey Him, the more we know. Only love makes God real and brings Him to us. That's the biblical theory of knowledge, a way of knowing that is hidden from the wise and prudent and given to babes.

It seems to me that those of us who take the Bible straight are more inclined toward explanations than we are toward obedience. First we must understand the Bible, we say, and then we'll do it.

Truth does call for explanation, but not as much as we think or as much as we want. There is an order in the way God reveals Himself, and that order is inviolate: He speaks; we obey; He explains it—maybe. It's simply not true that God must explain everything to us before we can obey Him. He's not obligated to explain anything to us, and some things He can't explain until we get to heaven and have His pure heart.

More than a hundred years ago, revivalist Charles Finney issued a caution about trying to understand everything before we set out to obey. This practice, he said, would inevitably produce a critical, intellectual pride that "either has no real faith or holds most loosely to divine things that do not admit of a clear explanation." In other words, if I don't understand a particular text, I don't have to do what it tells me to do.

But Scripture teaches us that we must obey God's Word whether we understand it or not. We must bow before each word in humble submission. As T. S. Eliot taught us,

> You are not here to verify, . . .
> Or carry report. You are here to kneel.

When we kneel in worship and submission, then and only then do we begin to see. "Obedience," Tozer said, "is the opener of the eyes."

As you read a passage from the Scriptures, pause after each verse or phrase to hear what God is saying to you. Consider how to practice what you've read. Think about how other believers may have lived out this truth. Consider what may keep you from living out the truth yourself.

As you sense your inability to obey some truth, come before God humbly and tell Him how helpless you are. Ask Him to live His life in you and to do all that you cannot do. He will finish the work that He has called you to do.

Sometimes I speak to men who tell me they don't understand the Bible. They're looking for a method that will shed more light on the text.

I rarely suggest a method, though there are many, because methodology is hardly ever the issue. I rather remind these men of something Peter said: "Rid yourselves of all malice and all deceit, hypocrisy, envy, and slander of every kind. Like newborn babies, crave pure spiritual milk, so that by it you may grow up in your salvation" (1 Peter 2:1–2).

Peter's analogy is easy to follow: Hunger is a natural condition for healthy children. It's sickness that takes away their appetite. If we obey what we already know of God's Word—rid ourselves of the pathogens of malice, deceit, hypocrisy, envy, and slander—we will understand what we have read, and we will develop a hunger for more.

If you find confusion in your mind, it may be that there's some evil thing in your heart, some unrepaired wrong. "Those who by insincerity and falsehood close their deeper eyes are incapable of using the more superficial eyes of their understanding," George MacDonald said.

What's the solution? Read the Word with your heart wide open. Let God speak to the insincerity and subterfuge in you. Let Him prove and delve into your pride, avarice, greed, hateful thoughts, resentful grudges, indifference to human need. Let Him disinter every buried secret and reveal every dark thought. Permit Him to speak to every harmful habit, every bad attitude, every troubling perspective, every destructive way of relating to others. "Let there be no delay," John Wesley said. "Whatever you resolve begin to execute the first moment you can."

But here I must issue a caution: Seek the will of God with a resolution to do it, but seek to do it through His grace alone. *Grace* is the operative word. It is grace and grace alone that "teaches us to say 'No' to ungodliness and worldly passions, and to live self-controlled, upright and godly lives in this present age" (Titus 2:12). Obedience, to the extent that any of us obey, is God's gift to us.

One thing more: When you get understanding, be sure to give it away as soon as possible. Otherwise it will go to your head.

—In Quietness and Confidence

Maturely Handling the Word of Truth

Present yourself to God as one approved,
a workman who does not need to be ashamed and who
correctly handles the word of truth.
—2 Timothy 2:15

Most of us are biblically educated beyond our character, perhaps because we confuse the means with the end. We falsely assume that the purpose of Bible study is mere learning, a fallacy particularly characteristic of those of us who take the Bible straight.

But mere orthodoxy is never enough. Even the demons are orthodox (James 2:19). They study the Bible too. They make their own prophetic charts and draw their own theological lines, but the Book doesn't alter their behavior. They're devilish to the end.

In 2 Timothy 2:15 the word Paul used that is translated "who correctly handles" means "one who goes for a goal." Classical Greek writers used the word of road builders who cut their way straight through a forest to a predetermined location. The Septuagint (the first Greek translation of the Old Testament) used the word in the last phrase of Proverbs 3:6:

> In all your ways acknowledge him,
>> and he will make your paths straight [direct you to the goal].

Paul contrasted good Bible study with the flawed methods of those who were "quarreling about words," which, he said, "is of no value, and only ruins those who listen" (2 Timothy 2:14). Further, "godless chatter"—mere discussion of the Bible without the goal of godliness—will make one become "more and more ungodly" (2:16). Ironically God's Word, when misused, can make us less and less like God!

Paul therefore warns Timothy to "flee the evil desires of youth" (2:22), a command that in context has little or nothing to do with youthful sexual desires. Paul rather had in mind the wrong-headed passion of the young and the immature to argue about meaning—*word-fight* is the term he coins. Those who mishandle God's Word in this way are workmen who ought to be ashamed.

Instead of arguing about meaning, Timothy was to "pursue righteousness, faith, love and peace, along with those who call on the Lord out of a pure heart" (2:22). In other words, he was to seek God and His goodness through the Book. To do so is to handle the Word correctly—to go straight to the goal.

The purpose of Bible study is clear. It ought to produce worship and make us more and more like our Lord. To the extent that we read the Scriptures for that reason, our Bible reading is valid; to the extent that we do not, it's nonproductive. Worse, it's counterproductive, making us less and less like our Lord. Thus hymnist Mary Lathbury prayed:

> Beyond the sacred page, I seek Thee, Lord;
> My spirit pants for Thee, O living Word!
>
> *—The Strength of a Man*

We Know in Part

My heart is not proud, O Lord,
*   my eyes are not haughty;*
I do not concern myself with great matters
*   or things too wonderful for me.*
But I have stilled and quieted my soul;
*   like a weaned child with its mother,*
*   like a weaned child is my soul within me.*
O Israel, put your hope in the Lord
*   both now and forevermore.*

—Psalm 131

Carolyn was trying to help Sarah, one of our granddaughters, become a little less dogmatic. You see, Sarah is certain about everything. The issue, as I recall, had something to do with whether the movie *The Lion King* was available as a video. Sarah was sure that it was, and she said so.

Carolyn, trying to set a good example, replied softly, "Sarah, I may be wrong, but I don't think it's out in video yet." "Yes, Nana," Sarah replied, "You *are* wrong!"

Sarah's assertiveness is kid stuff. She's only six and young enough to be too sure of herself. As we grow up, however, we usually become less certain. Too much of life is beyond our ken.

Paul said, "We know in part" (1 Corinthians 13:9), and I suppose we always will. Even in heaven when perfection has come, the joy of discovery will surely continue. We won't know everything there is to know there; we'll be taught of God and learning—learning better and faster, I assume—going "further up and further in," as C. S. Lewis said.

(I once remarked to a friend that we might not have Bibles in heaven because we'll be taught by God Himself and won't need them there, to which he replied, "Then what will we Christians have to argue about?")

We have an English word, *weird*, that refers to things that are odd or strange. The word is derived from an Old English word, *wyrd*, which meant something a little different: It had to do with things that were unaccountably mysterious and uncanny and better left that way.

We don't allow much *wyrd* these days, at least in the circles I frequent. We have a place for everything and everything is in its place. All things are neat and tidy and tucked away.

I must say, however, that a lot of my certainty has begun to evaporate lately, simply because I don't understand as much as I used to. It's not that I lack conviction about the reality of God, but rather I've come to see that in my attempts to explain Him I'm mostly in the dark. His ways are "beyond [my] understanding" (Job 36:26).

One of the church fathers, Ireneaus, pointed out that the essential difference between orthodoxy and heresy is that orthodoxy is rooted in paradox and mystery. Heresy, on the other hand, is rooted in clarity and precision. I find a lot of wisdom in those words.

I used to have clear and precise explanations for most things, but when I finally got around to thinking about my explanations, it occurred to me that I really didn't know what I was talking about. I had the right words, but I didn't know what the words meant.

Now I don't know as much as I used to. In fact, as I often say to Carolyn, I find myself believing more and more ardently in fewer and fewer things.

It came to me one day that my mind was much too busy and argumentative to know the peace of God. Always reasoning and worrying—I had no time to cultivate that silence in which God speaks. The main thing for me now is not to know all the answers, but to know God, made real and personal in Jesus. What I hunger for is a purer vision of Him through His Word and a greater love for Him. Theories about when, where, how, and why don't bother me much anymore. Oh, I think about such things from time to time, but they don't hang me up the way they used to.

I like the portrait David paints of himself in Psalm 131.

This isn't Nirvana's "never mind," but rather the thoughts of a man who has his mind right—no longer restless, searching, craving, struggling with the mysteries of life, but quietly abiding in his Father's love.

I pray often for David's spirit and for the realization that only a few things are necessary—as Jesus put it, really "only one" (Luke 10:42 NASB).

"But," a friend of mine once observed, "questions imply answers. If God put questions in our minds, doesn't He have the answers in His?"

Of course He does, but we don't have to have the answers—that's the point. We can live with paradox and mystery. We can know "in part" and be comfortable with not knowing the whole.

"But doesn't God draw lines?" you ask. Indeed, He does. He draws straight lines, but they're "pure" lines, as George MacDonald said, "without breadth and consequently sometimes invisible to mortal eyes." (MacDonald was thinking here of theological lines. God's *moral* lines are very clear.)

Those lines—theological lines that sometimes divide us—are most often lines that aren't meant to be noticed at all. They're better taken lightly or set aside if we can't see them well.

I often think of this idea—that some of God's lines are drawn invisibly—these days when I sit down to write. It has made me more reticent when I write and I hope a little more humble, lest my writings merely add to the sum total of ignorance in this world. That would be a futile achievement.

Theologian Karl Barth imagined entering heaven with a pushcart full of his books and hearing the angels chuckle. "In heaven," he said, "I shall dump even the *Church Dogmatics* [his primary work] . . . on some heavenly floor as a pile of waste paper."

Furthermore, the fact that I know "in part" affects the way I look at other believers—especially those not exactly like me. Most things about which we disagree don't matter to me anymore.

It occurred to me one day, while reviewing our church doctrinal statement, that our assertions were so inclusive they were exclusive. It included a lot of things over which Christians have differed for centuries. I wondered why we included them. Augustine, John Calvin, Martin Luther, and a host of other heroes could not have enjoyed our fellowship. Our creed, which sheltered us so well, would have stifled them.

Our honest desire to think accurately about God can move too easily into a conviction that our doctrinal statements contain everything there is to know about God, which, in turn, has the effect of reducing God to our creed. Without humble uncertainty, our statements can evolve into hard dogma that isolates us from one another. Certainty can breed intolerance. "No one damns like the orthodox," as they say.

Modes of baptism, forms of church government, versions of the Bible, end-time scenarios—issues that have been up for grabs from the beginning—become the main things, the distinctives that divide us physically, emotionally, and spiritually. The whole business makes me sad.

In our efforts to give away our faith, we must, in the midst of our certainty about some things, humbly acknowledge the mystery of all things. We're dealing with matters we don't fully understand; in truth, we know very little about God.

This means we don't have to have all the answers. We can be awed and perplexed. We can be befuddled. We can be at a loss for words. We can say, "I don't understand this, but . . ." We can even be silent.

In his book *The Trivialization of God,* Donald McCullough, former president of San Francisco Theological Seminary, said that humility should so encompass our statements about God that we are driven to speak "with the tone of a high school sophomore telling what she knows about vectors to a Nobel prize-winning physicist. What we say may be true enough, but so obviously spoken out of ignorance that we dare not chatter on in blissful confidence. Perhaps," McCullough goes on to say, "it is time for a deferential hush."

Finally, this understanding—that we know very little—has something to say about the way we look at our own growth in grace. The main thing is not to know more things, but to live out the things we know: to love the Lord our God with all our heart, soul, and mind and follow Him in grateful obedience. We do not need to know the secrets of God. We just need to love Him and do what He shows us to do.

At the end of his life, Paul said that he had only one thought: "to know Christ and the power of his resurrection and the fellowship of sharing in his sufferings, becoming like him in his death" (Philippians 3:10). That just about says it all.

I recall hearing a story about that wonderful saint John Newton, whose mind, as he aged, began to fail. "I recall but two things now," he said. "I am a great sinner and my Jesus is a great Savior."

It's a blessing, I think, that we forget most of what we once knew. I can hardly wait for that day.

—In Quietness and Confidence

Killing Me Softly

My lover spoke and said to me,
  "Arise, my darling,
    my beautiful one, and come with me.
See! The winter is past;
    the rains are over and gone.
Flowers appear on the earth;
    the season of singing has come,
the cooing of doves
    is heard in our land.
The fig tree forms its early fruit;
    the blossoming vines spread their fragrance.
Arise, come, my darling;
    my beautiful one, come with me."
                              —Song of Songs 2:10–13

In the Song of Songs, Shulamite the bride cries out, "Oh, that he would kiss me." Is this not the thing for which our souls hunger as well—to be gathered in, to be smothered by the loving "kisses" of God?[2]

Saint Bernard of Clairvaux wrote, "O happy kiss, and wonder of amazing self-humbling which is not a mere meeting of lips, but the union of God with

---

2. All souls are feminine. Not female but *feminine*. (The word for "soul" is feminine in Hebrew.) In the Song of Songs it is the groom and not the bride who symbolizes God, the bride and not the groom who symbolizes the soul. The reason for this is not that males are in any way superior and more "godlike," but that God, by His nature, is the husband of my soul, and I, by nature, am His bride. This is symbolic language, of course.

man." Bernard urges us to call out to God with the words of the bride: "Take me away with you—let us hurry!"

Though human lovers can sing the Song of Songs to each other, here we find it employed as a means of worship to God. This is a way the Song can be read and has been read for centuries. Thus, on one level it is a description of the purest human love we can imagine, but on a deeper level it reflects our love for God and His unfathomable love for us.

C. I. Scofield wrote, "Nowhere in Scripture does the unspiritual mind tread upon ground so mysterious and incomprehensible as in this book, while the saintliest men and women of the ages have found it a source of pure and exquisite delight. That the love of the divine Bridegroom should follow all the analogies of the marriage relation seems evil only to minds so ascetic that marital desire itself seems to them unholy."

Here is the synthesis, I believe, between modern writers who interpret the Song literally and traditionalists who interpret the Song as merely symbolic. We can cut across these either/or positions and rightly interpret it both/and, because all human love is a symbol and sign of a deeper human hunger for eternal love. We may deny that it exists, but in our quieter moments we *know* it is true.

Everything is about love, or the lack of it, or so we say; but *human* love is not the ultimate end that we seek. It is but the means to that end, the stimulus that triggers in us a deep thirst for God's absolute and consuming love. We are never satisfied with the affection we're given here on earth, no matter how intense and enduring it may be. We seek something more than one another.

"Love is a journey to another land," said Anglo-Irish writer Rebecca West. She was wiser than she knew, for, put another way, romantic love and natural affections are meant to set us on a journey to find infinite love. As though we're following a river upstream, we pursue love's meandering course to its headwaters. There, at its source (God's effervescent love), we find the spring from which all human loves flow. There we find "a spring of water welling up to eternal life" (John 4:14) from which we can slack our thirst forever. This "is the end of the heart's quest and the beginning of its fullness," Aquinas said.

This, I believe, is why human love and sexual passion permeate and dominate our lives. It is God's gift to us to draw us to His everlasting love. Our passion is more than physical impulse or instinct; it is a God-designed reflection, however pale, of our passion to know Him and to be known by Him. It is no coincidence that sexual intercourse in the Bible is described as "know-ing," for human sexual passion is a small representation of the chief end of man to "know God and enjoy Him forever."

Long ago Charles Williams noted that "sensuality and sanctity are so closely intertwined they can hardly be separated." Paul said as much: "For this reason a man will leave his father and mother and be united to his wife, and the two will become one flesh [another term for sexual intimacy]." Then he concludes with this thought: "This [sexual union] is a profound mystery— but *I am [also] talking about Christ and the church*" (Ephesians 5:31–32).

Here Paul clearly links marital sexual intimacy with spiritual intimacy with God. One is a representation and reflection of the other. Thus, I say, *sex is holy,* an eloquent expression of our profound, inexpressible hunger for God, a passionate urge to merge with the object of our love and ultimately with the God who loves us as no human lover can.

That longing—to know God and experience His love—originates with God. It is His calling, His wooing that awakens us to desire. Indeed, we would not seek Him if He did not first seek us. Our longing for intimacy and union is the answering cry of our hearts to His call. "Even when men knock on the door of a brothel," said G. K. Chesterton, "they are looking for God." That hunger may be masked and distorted and misunderstood, but it is undeniably there.

This marital love and sex is good, but not as good as it gets, which is why God has placed limits on the depth of all human relationships. Our need for intimacy always outstrips the capacity of another human being to satisfy it. We will always betray another's love in one way or another. This is what Original Sin means: No one is completely trustworthy; no one will always "keep covenant." We will always let one another down.

"An image can easily become an idol and romantic love is a powerful im-age," wrote Peter Kreeft in *Three Philosophies of Life.* "We expect joy from this human experience, but it ends in bitter disappointment. We have heaped on the shoulders of our beloved a burden of joy-making only God can carry and we are scandalized when those shoulders break."

That hunger—for something beyond human love—is the way God leads us to His love. In each of us there is a deep and holy place reserved for Him alone, a place that no one else, not even the greatest human lover, can ever fill. We draw near to God to find final affection.

May I suggest a journey, then, an exploration? Read each poem in the

Song of Songs at a leisurely pace and put yourself in it. Meditate on each line. Make Shulamite's words your words and offer them up to God. Then read Solomon's (the lover's) words as God's words to you and listen to His response. Hear Him speak to your heart, "Come away with Me, My one, My bride." The longer we stay with the symbol and reflect upon it, the more it will yield. "A symbol should go on deepening," said Flannery O'Connor in *The Habit of Being.*

Imagine! God wants *you,* not for your body, your clothes, your talent, your intellect, your personality, but simply because you are you! He loves *you.* He cannot take His eyes from *you.*

"Ah," you say. "How could He love poor me? I am dark with sin and guilt, loathsome, grotesque." No, you are His "perfect one" (Song 6:9). He sees awesome beauty in you.

"Love is blind," you say. No, *infatuation* is blind, but not God's love. He sees you as you are, yet He sings to you.

> My dove in the clefts of the rock,
>> in the hiding places on the mountainside,
> show me your face,
>> let me hear your voice;
> for your voice is sweet,
>> and your face is lovely (Song of Songs 2:14).

Is this illusion? No, it is clear-sighted love. God's eyes are filled with your beauty. He loved you before your father, spouse, or children loved you (or wounded you). "If you were the only person on earth, He would have gone to all the trouble He went to just to win *you,*" one early Christian writer said. Does this not excite us?

Whatever your heart may be saying at this moment, you must know that God is the lover of your soul. Even now, in your unperfected state, He cries out to you, "How beautiful you are . . . how beautiful."

We are special objects of God's favor and affection. His is a love that swallows up every love in its fullness. The Song in this way becomes more than a love song. It becomes adoration and worship.

—Song of a Longing Heart

PART 2

Pursuing Righteousness and Faith

Reflecting God's Righteousness

This is how the birth of Jesus Christ came about:
His mother Mary was pledged to be married to Joseph,
but before they came together, she was found to be with child
through the Holy Spirit. Because Joseph her husband was a
righteous man and did not want to expose her to public disgrace,
he had in mind to divorce her quietly.
—Matthew 1:18–19

We mostly spend [our] lives conjugating three verbs: to Want, to
Have, and to Do. Craving, clutching, and fussing, on the material,
political, social, emotional, intellectual—even on the religious—
plane, we are kept in perpetual unrest: forgetting that none of
these verbs have any ultimate significance, except so far as they
are transcended by and included in, the fundamental verb, to Be:
and that Being, not wanting, having and doing, is the essence of a
spiritual life.
—Evelyn Underhill

Joseph, the husband of Mary, is a dim figure in the background of the Christmas drama. He drops offstage almost immediately and is never heard of again. And he is known for one thing alone: He was "a righteous [good] man."

Joseph was a man in whom mercy triumphed over justice. When he discovered that Mary was pregnant, though he could have shamed her and saved himself a good deal of embarrassment, he chose to shield her from disgrace. (A good man would never humiliate anyone, especially the woman he loves.)

Joseph was a man who, though he could not quite grasp the immensity of what was going on around him, was quick to respond to what he perceived to be the will of God.

Joseph was a man whose mercy translated into a strong, enduring love for Mary that transcended self-interest; a man who left everything—home, country, and business—and fled to Egypt to save Mary and the baby Jesus.

In our Scripture record, Joseph never utters a word—not one word, not one syllable, not one sound—yet he speaks to us today.

Where are those Joseph-men today? Men who are authentically and transparently good? Why are they so few? Good old boys come and go, but good men are much harder to find.

Finding work is more highly valued than being good these days, or so it seems to me. We hustle through life in the hope that if we do something long enough and well enough—and make enough money—we'll be worth something someday. That's why when we meet an individual for the first time, we usually ask, "What do you do?" For what a person *does* is what matters most, or so we seem to believe. The better question is the one we ask small children, "When you grow up, what do you want to *be*?"

Most of us want to *be* something, but first we have to *do*: We have a career to manage, money to make, a ministry to carry out—miles to go and promises to keep. That's our besetting, beguiling sin: always chasing after that elusive "something more." One more deal to make, one more hill to climb, one more challenge to overcome, one more program to enact. But as Thoreau would warn us, such preoccupation leads to a life of quiet desperation, be it healthy, wealthy, or otherwise.

The better course is to "seek first his [God's] kingdom and his righteousness," as Jesus said, for one quest leads inexorably to the other (Matthew 6:33).

When we design our days to make time for God, we reflect each day a little more of His righteousness. And the time to begin is right now. "How we spend our days is how we spend our hours," said Annie Dillard. "What we do with *this* hour is what we are doing."

—*Out of the Ordinary*

Abiding in Christ

I am the vine; you are the branches.
If a man remains in me and I in him, he will bear much fruit;
apart from me you can do nothing.
—John 15:5

There's an old vineyard in a canyon that I fish through now and then. It was an effort by some Idaho pioneer to grow grapes and make sweet wine I suppose, but it's long since been abandoned.

I saw it again this winter, and though the gnarled old stocks looked dead to me, I knew next spring they'd leaf out again and produce grapes. Through all the years, its fruit remains.

That old vineyard always reminds me of Jesus' metaphor found in John 15. When Jesus said, "I am the vine," He and His disciples were making their way down the east slope of Mount Zion—down the steps that led into the Valley of the Kidron on their way to the Mount of Olives. In that day the entire slope was one vast vineyard. The sight of the vines and the branches covered with spring blossoms and a late-working vine keeper or two probably evoked Jesus' metaphor.

Jesus saw the vine branches trained along trellises for vast distances, yet, as He knew, one life pervaded and sustained the whole from the oldest root to the farthest twig, leaf, and cluster. He thought of the connection between the vine and branch and the relationship His disciples sustained to Him and settled on this symbol.

We are branches, united to Jesus the vine, integrally joined to Him by faith and by God's goodness and grace. His life pervades our being from one end to the other. All that He has is ours for the taking. The result, Jesus insists, is "fruit."

The word *fruit* in the Bible rarely symbolizes souls brought to Christ. Rather it represents personal righteousness—not what we do but what we *are* (compare Isaiah 5:1–7; Galatians 5:22–23). Fruit, in the natural and biblical sense, is product of the life of the vine, penetrating and perfusing the branches so that something useful is produced. There can be no fruit apart from the vine. As Jesus said, "Without me you can do nothing."

We cannot by moral effort become fruitful. It is the result of daily association with Jesus. It begins with "abiding." Abiding is utter dependence—drawing on Christ for all that we do. It means sitting at His feet in solitude and surrender, listening for His voice, asking for His counsel, waiting for His impulses in intercession and action, then walking through the world trusting, resting, asking for His help.

Abiding is acknowledging our inadequacy and our inability to change ourselves one iota. It is a moment-by-moment yielding—not a fatalistic acquiescence or passive resignation, but an active submission of our whole being to Jesus so that His presence and power can be released through our bodies in every circumstance. It is an open receptivity that undergirds all we do.

The result, Jesus says, is fruit—"love, joy, peace, patience, kindness, goodness, faithfulness, gentleness and self-control"—those infused virtues that produce refreshment and healing in others.

Busy lives revolt against abiding. When we allow ourselves to be swept up in every cause and concern, when we surrender to every demand, when we give ourselves to every worthwhile project, when we try to be all things to all people all the time, we have no time to abide—and then we become useless. Like broken and detached branches we wither and die and are good for nothing.

Frenzy destroys the fruit because it disconnects us from the root—that source of goodness and wisdom that marks us and makes us useful. We must be less busy—to take time to be joined to Jesus, that, as F. B. Meyer said, "He may produce in and through us whatever fruit He will for the nourishment of men and the glory of God."

—In Quietness and Confidence

Trust and the Will of God

Now listen, you who say, "Today or tomorrow we will go to this or that city, spend a year there, carry on business and make money." Why, you do not even know what will happen tomorrow. What is your life? You are a mist that appears for a little while and then vanishes. Instead, you ought to say, "If it is the Lord's will, we will live and do this or that."
—James 4:13–15

Planning is something we do every day, a necessary effort to make the most of our time here on earth. Without an intelligent plan, disorder and chaos overwhelm us.

Yet James insists that planning can be "evil" (his word, not mine) if we plan without making room for God. Why? Because it's presumptuous to assume that we have that much control over our lives. How can we presume to mark our calendars one year hence when we don't know what the next moment will bring? How can we plan so confidently for tomorrow when we may not be here when it comes?

You are a mist, says James, a vapor, a puff of smoke, a flitting cloud, a breath ("breath and britches," my mother used to say). Here today, gone tomorrow. A vagrant virus, an inadvertent stumble, a stray bullet, an errant motorist strikes us down or takes us out. We're completely at the mercy of our circumstances.

Yet circumstance is not chance. There are no random happenings, no uncaused events. The various fortunes of life are in God's hands. That's why we ought to say, "If the Lord wills I will do this or that." Anything else is playing God.

Here James is concerned with what theologians call *providence*. The term comes from two Latin words *pro* and *videre*, meaning "to look ahead" and thus "to plan in advance" and finally "to carry out the plan." And since the agent of providence is an all-knowing, all-powerful God whom nothing and no one can resist, literally *everything* is included in His plan.

There is no cause other than God. His wisdom is the reason for everything and His power the means by which everything is carried out. There are no accidents, no flukes, no fortuities, no maverick molecules, no loose ends. "There is no neutral ground in the universe," C. S. Lewis says. "Every square inch, every split second is claimed by God."

If you have trouble with this assertion, I suggest you simply read the Scriptures and let them make their own impression on you. (Take, for example, Psalm 139 and David's insistence that everything about him had been worked out in God's mind long before it was worked into his DNA.) You'll find that the writers express the thought of God's sovereignty repeatedly and incisively, but the assurance with which they express it, or simply assume it, should have an even more convincing effect.

The biblical writers were not fools. They saw the problem inherent in God's sovereignty and human free will. They understood they were dealing with issues that appeared to be conflictive and inexplicable, yet they did not stumble over apparent contradiction, nor did they try to reconcile what appear to be disparate facts. They simply asserted our moral responsibility in *all* things and God's control over *all* things and moved on.

This is not the place to delve into this issue; it's enough to say at this point that there is no contradiction in God, only paradox and enigma. And the closer we get to our Lord, the more paradoxical and enigmatic things begin to appear. We should expect that to be so. "If I knew of a theory in which was never an uncompleted arch or turret," George MacDonald wrote, "in whose circling wall was never a breach, that theory I should know but to avoid: such gaps are the eternal windows through which the dawn shall look in."

Infinite wisdom is something other than knowing more than finite beings; it is wisdom in another dimension and thus wisdom beyond our ken. All we can say is what the biblical writers so eloquently and explicitly say: Despite our freedom, God is in *complete* control. Beyond that we cannot go.

Naturally, if some god is substituted other than the God and Father of our Lord Jesus Christ, this doctrine would be unspeakably cruel, but providence is far more than *kismet*—fate—or impersonal, rigid control. Infinite love and wisdom lie behind every circumstance. If only we had eyes to see it, we would discover a loving and powerful Savior at work in every moment of our history and in every experience of our life—even in our sleep, our idle moments, and our play—turning us into glorious, winsome sons and daughters that He will enjoy forever.

Paul puts it this way: "We know that in all things [and he means *all* things] God works for the good of those who love him, who have been called according to his purpose. For those God foreknew he also predestined to be conformed to the likeness of his Son" (Romans 8:28–29).

Paul is not suggesting that all things are good, or ought to feel good, but that all things are working for *our* good, the good for which we were created—to be just like God's own dear Son.

So must we forgo all long-range planning and simply go with the flow? No, we can make our plans and dream our dreams, but we must do so fully aware of God's kindly and purposeful control. We "live and do this or that" as *He* wills and works out His durable, eternal purpose for us.

My friend Jim Catlin recently described a friend of his who had his life well mapped out: "I had to say to him," Jim wrote, "that life is seldom that linear, that predictable, and in light of God's sovereign plans for us, that discernible. We have an obligation, no, a *privilege*, of exercising any capacity that God has given us to plan ahead, but ultimately we must give a nod of sovereignty to the One who *sees* the road ahead."

God's will is my safety—to know that I'm not on my own, to know that no matter what I plan I am *always* in God's plans. I can cast all my anxiety on Him because He is caring for me.

To quote that peaceful angler Izaac Walton: "When I would beget content and increase confidence in the providence of Almighty God, I will walk the meadows by some gliding stream, and there contemplate the lilies and other little dumb creatures for which God plans and cares and therefore trust in Him."

The word *trust,* they tell me, is an old contraction of the superlative degree of *true* (true, truer, truest). Trust knows that God is incomparably true when He tells us that all things—even those things that seem wrong or regressive—are determined for our ultimate, eternal good.

—Growing Slowly Wise

Walking the Dark Valley

Even though I walk
*   through the valley of the shadow of death,*
I will fear no evil,
*   for you are with me;*
your rod and your staff,
*   they comfort me.*

—Psalm 23:4

I remember the impression I had as a child when I first heard the words "the valley of the shadow of death." I conjured up a mental picture of a storm-shrouded landscape, a yawning abyss at my feet, broken crags, precipitous cliffs, and a narrow, twisting footpath along narrow ledges, leading inexorably into thickening gloom below. The picture is locked in my mind.

The phrase *shadow of death* is actually one word in Hebrew meaning "deep darkness." It's a dreary word, used elsewhere in the Bible to describe the impenetrable darkness before creation (Amos 5:8), the thick darkness of a mine shaft (Job 28:3), and the black hole that is the abode of the dead (Job 10:21; 38:17). It's a word associated with anxiety and unfocused dread.

In *The Pilgrim's Progress* John Bunyan captured something of the terror of the place when he described it as "dark as pitch," inhabited by "hobgoblins, satyrs, dragons of the pit and fiends." A way "set full of pits, pitfalls, deep holes and shelvings." In the midst of the valley was "the mouth of hell."

The valley of the shadow of death is usually associated with the end of life, but Bunyan places it in the middle, where it rightly belongs. In fact there is not one valley; there are many, falling between the pastures where we find intermittent rest. There's no way around them. "We must go through many

72

hardships to enter the kingdom of God," Paul insisted (Acts 14:22). The desolate places are an inevitable and necessary part of the journey.

The valleys bring to mind the day an employer said "clean out your desk"; when a doctor said "your baby will never be normal"; when you found the stash in your son's closet; when your teenage daughter told you she was pregnant; when the doctor said you had cancer; when your spouse said he or she had no energy left to put into the relationship. Those are the dark days when we lose all perspective, when we say in despair, "It's no use; I can't go on."

The valleys are emblematic of periods of prolonged failure when we're shamed and broken by the full weight of the darkness within us; when we experience the isolation of despair, the exhausted aftermath of self-gratification and spent vice; when we feel unalterably defiled and wonder if we will ever regain our sense of worth.

The valleys symbolize those dreary days of deep loneliness when we say with David,

> No one is concerned for me.
> I have no refuge;
> > no one cares for my life (Psalm 142:4).

Even God seems aloof and remote; there's an unaccountable chill in the air. We cry out with David,

> My God, my God, why have you forsaken me?
> Why are you so far from saving me,
> > so far from the words of my groaning?
> O my God, I cry out by day, but you do not answer (Psalm 22:1–2).

I used to think that life was mostly green pasture with an occasional dark valley along the way, but now I realize it's the other way around. There are days of surprising joy, but much of life is a vale of tears. Every year confirms my belief that life is indeed difficult and demanding. Any other view of life is escapist.

The path by which God takes us often seems to lead away from our good, causing us to believe we've missed a turn and taken the wrong road. That's because most of us have been taught to believe that if we're on the right track, God's goodness will always translate into earthly good: that He'll heal, deliver, and exempt us from disease and pain; that we'll have money in the bank, kids who turn out well, nice clothes, a comfortable living, and a leisurely retirement. In that version of life everyone turns out to be a winner; nobody loses a business, fails in marriage, or lives in poverty.

But that's a pipe dream far removed from the biblical perspective that God's love often leads us down roads where earthly comforts fail us so He can give us eternal consolation (2 Thessalonians 2:16). "Suffering ripens our souls," said Aleksander Solzhenitsyn.

God doesn't cushion the journey; He lets life jolt us. As F. B. Meyer said, if we've been told that we're supposed to be on a bumpy track, every jolt along the way simply confirms the fact that we're still on the right road.

When we come to the end of all valleys, we'll understand that every path has been selected out of all possible options for our ultimate good. God, in fact, could not have taken us by any other way. No other route would have been as safe and as certain as the one by which we came. And if only we could see the path as God has always seen it, we would select it as well.

God is with us, walking everywhere *incognito,* as C. S. Lewis said. "And the incognito is not always hard to penetrate. The real labor is to remember, to attend. In fact, to come awake. Still more, to remain awake." The main thing to remember is to make ourselves think about His presence; to acknowledge that He is with us, as real as He was in the days of His flesh when He walked with His disciples amid the sorrows and haunts of this world.

Difficulty and drudgery make us think of ourselves as being all alone, but He has said, "I will never leave you nor forsake you." Of Him alone it can be said, He will never say goodbye.

Ultimately the dark valleys can make God more real to us than ever before. "God becomes a reality," Richard Foster said, "when he becomes a necessity." How many times have I heard from those who have endured intense suffering that the experience of their pain pulled them away from idolatries and eventually enlarged their intimacy with their Shepherd, which is what brings us peace and unimaginable joy.

We're inclined to fix on the valley and its pain, but God chooses to look forward and anticipate its effect. He deals with our divided hearts through disappointment, grief, and tears, weaning us from other loves and passions and centering us on Him. We learn to trust Him in the darkness; when all that is left is the sound of His voice and the knowledge that He is near; when all we can do is slip our hand into His and feel "the familiar clasp of things divine." These are times that wean us away from sensuality—that tendency to live by feelings rather than by faith in God's unseen presence. We become independent of places and moods and content with God alone.

The dark days cause us to enter into a very special relationship with our Lord. As Job said,

> My ears had heard of you
> but now my eyes have *seen* you (Job 42:5).

There are glimpses of God that can only be revealed when earthly joy has ceased.

David himself understood the adversity that draws us to God's heart. Subjected to neglect by his mother and father and demeaned by the rest of his family, he was deeply scarred. His family would have ruined him if he had not fled to his heavenly Father for refuge. Out of his loneliness and heartache David wrote,

> Though my father and mother forsake me,
> the Lord will receive me (Psalm 27:10).

David was hammered and hurt throughout his entire life, every blow converting him, exposing his ambivalence, until he would finally cry,

> Surely I was sinful at birth,
> sinful from the time my mother conceived me . . .
> Create in me a pure [undivided] heart, O God (Psalm 51:5, 10).

God's work is never done. As F. B. Meyer said: "Thus always—the rod, the stripes, the chastisements; but amid all, the love of God, carrying out His redemptive purpose, never hasting, never resting, never forgetting, but making all things work together until the evil is eliminated and the soul is purified."

Then David cried out, "My soul finds rest in God *alone*" (Psalm 62:1). It was through darkness, suffering, and pain that all David's passions were integrated into one.

And so all of life is consummated in loving God. That's what we were made for; that's where ultimate satisfaction lies. If that's true, and I firmly believe it is, then although it is often hard to do, we should welcome any valley that leads us to Him.

One thing more: No valley goes on forever. We walk *through* the valley of the shadow of death. God knows what we can endure. He will not let us be tempted or tested beyond what we can bear (1 Corinthians 10:13). The deliverance we seek may be subject to delay, but we must never doubt that our day will come.

> Weeping may remain for a night,
>   but rejoicing comes in the morning (Psalm 30:5).

Sorrow has its time to be, but God will mitigate the tears when their work is done. Those who mourn will be comforted. There will be an end.

—*Psalm 23*

Seeing God

Open my eyes that I may see.
—Psalm 119:18

The best stories begin with God: "The Lord said to him [Elijah], 'Go back the way you came, and go to the Desert of Damascus. When you get there, anoint Hazael king over Aram. Also, anoint Jehu son of Nimshi king over Israel, and anoint Elisha son of Shaphat from Abel Meholah to succeed you as prophet' " (1 Kings 19:15–16).

And so, aware that his work on earth was almost finished, the old prophet Elijah turned again toward the land of Israel, to the village of Abel Meholah. The rest of 1 Kings 19 tells the story. There Elijah found Elisha, Shaphat's son, dutifully working the ground, "driving the twelfth" of twelve pairs of oxen, eating the dust of eleven plows that were turning the soil in front of him.

The old prophet slipped up behind the young man and cast his rough, camel-hair mantle over his shoulders and moved on. Not a word was spoken, but Elisha understood. "When a great teacher died," Sir John Malcolm wrote in his *History of Persia,* "he bequeathed his patched mantle to the disciple he most esteemed . . . His mantle was his all and its transfer marked out his heir." The mantle was a symbol of Elisha's call to the prophetic office.

Elisha's response was immediate: He left his oxen and "set out to follow Elijah." Thus his work began.

For a time Elisha did little more than minister to the physical needs of the old prophet, "pour[ing] water on his hands," as the idiom puts it (2 Kings 3:11). It was a time of humble, obscure service. But he learned at the feet of his master. He listened well, determined to let none of Elijah's words fall to the ground.

In turn, Elijah ministered to Elisha, strengthening the young man's grip on God. The old man knew there was no better way to spend his last days.

But earthly things must come to an end, and God informed Elijah that He was calling him home. Elijah, knowing that his departure was imminent and determined to leave a lasting legacy, asked his disciple, "What can I do for you before I am taken from you?" (2 Kings 2:9). It was a door flung wide open, a chancy *carte blanche*, yet Elijah knew that Elisha would not ask for anything that God would not bestow.

Elijah's confidence was well placed. Elisha's reply showed the stuff of which he was made. He sought neither prestige nor power but a "double portion" of Elijah's spirit.

What did Elisha want? To be considered Elijah's eldest son, heir to his influence and successor to his work, for the "double portion" was the inheritance of the firstborn son (Deuteronomy 21:17).

Elisha knew he would succeed Elijah in his work, but he knew he could not take on its responsibilities and face its perils without adequate resources. He was eager to seek the Spirit that had endowed the older prophet with power from on high, for Elisha knew that he was a mere man—weak and feckless apart from God. If he was to do the work God had called him to do, he must have all of God to do it.

Elijah replied, "If you see me when I am taken from you, it [the double portion] will be yours—otherwise not" (2 Kings 2:10). There was nothing arbitrary in this test. It was utterly suitable, for God's work requires the ability to "see."

And so, "As they were walking along and talking together, suddenly a chariot of fire and horses of fire appeared and separated the two of them, and Elijah went up to heaven in a whirlwind. Elisha saw this and cried out, 'My father! My father! The chariots and horsemen of Israel!' And Elisha saw him no more" (2 Kings 2:11–12).

Elijah's requirement that Elisha see his departure had to do with one's ability to see what cannot be seen. "Elijah was a man like us," James 5:17 says. His power came not from latent or inherent human ability, but because his eyes were fixed "on what is unseen" (2 Corinthians 4:18). That was the secret of his influence. The issue in Elijah's "test" was whether Elisha had learned that secret.

An ordinary man or woman standing in that place would have seen nothing but the sudden disappearance of the prophet. As F. B. Meyer noted in his book *Elijah and the Secret of His Power,* "To senses dulled by passion or blinded by materialism, the space occupied by the flaming seraphim would have seemed devoid of any special interest and bare as the rest of the surrounding scenery." But Elisha, an extraordinary man, saw the invisible hosts of God. He had learned from Elijah to fix his eyes "on what is unseen." This was the secret of his enduring influence.

And so it is with us. There is a world that "lies around us like a cloud; a world we do not see," noted Harriet Beecher Stowe, another realm of reality, more actual, more substantial than anything we can see, hear, touch, taste, smell in this world. Faith is the means by which we gain access to this invisible world. It is to the spiritual realm what the five senses are to the natural; it is the means by which we grasp spiritual reality and bring it into the realm of our experience. Our goal, then, is to "grow eyes," to borrow a phrase from George MacDonald.

And how do we grow eyes?

Simply put, "seeing" is believing. Seeing is *faith*, pure and simple. "Faith is being . . . sure of what we do not see" (Hebrews 11:1). "By faith, [Moses] left Egypt, not fearing the king's anger; he persevered because he *saw him who is invisible*" (Hebrews 11:27). Faith is the indispensable element in all our work for God. Without it we can do nothing.

Faith cannot be generated. It is a gift of God given in answer to prayer. Do you want to "see" God in all His glory? Pray that the eyes of your hearts may be enlightened that you may see . . . (see Ephesians 1:18).

Faith grows as we feed on God's Word: "Faith comes from hearing the message, and the message is heard through the word of Christ" (Romans 10:17). Spiritual awareness is seeing everything through God's eyes, hearing with His ears. The test of our time in the Word of God is this: Has it enabled us to see?

Faith is the product of obedience. Our sense of God's presence is conditioned by the purity of our hearts. "What you see," C. S. Lewis wrote, "depends a good deal on . . . what sort of person you are." It is the pure in heart who "see God" (Matthew 5:8).

What's needed is an undivided and uncompromising devotion to Christ, singleness and simplicity of purpose to love Him and follow Him. "Purity of heart is to will one thing," Kierkegaard said, and that one thing is God's will. Uncontaminated devotion to Christ is the source of insight into the unseen world. It enables perceptions that others cannot achieve. Such men and women glimpse the workings of God where others detect *nothing*.

Lord, open our eyes that we may *see* . . . (Psalm 119:18).

                                                    —*Seasoned with Salt*

On the Mountain of the Lord

Take your son, your only son, Isaac, whom you love, and go to
the region of Moriah. Sacrifice him there as a burnt offering on
one of the mountains I will tell you about.
—Genesis 22:2

After decades of difficulty, Abraham was at last settling into the good life. Ishmael, who had caused so much trouble in the family, had gone off to start a new life. Abraham and Sarah had settled into godly ease and affluence and were enjoying their golden years with Isaac, their love and laughter.

One night the old man crawled into the sack and went off to sleep, oblivious to everything but thankfulness and joy—only to be awakened in the middle of the night by God's call.

This was *"the* God" as the text makes poignantly clear—the same God who had been so good to Abraham—who now delivers this awful line: "Take your *son.*"

Isaac was the promised one through whom God pledged to make Abraham great, the son who ensured his father's place in the world, Abraham's last hope. He had already lost one son, Ishmael. Would God take another? It made no sense at all.

Abraham knew that the gods of the Chaldeans and Canaanites demanded human sacrifice. How could he know at this juncture that his God would not demand his first-born? *Well,* Abraham must have thought, *it's come to this.*

Yet when morning came, despite his heartache and confusion, Abraham got up and got going, unlike me, inclined as I am to quibble with God when He asks me to do something disagreeable or dangerous. "Certainly not this?" I ask as I look for a loophole, some alternative to faith.

Not Abraham. He began to split wood for the fire, though every stroke must have driven the pain deeper into his heart. Then he saddled his donkey, loaded up the wood and other supplies, and went off with Isaac and two of his servants to a place only God knew—a mountain later called Moriah.

On the third day of his journey Abraham saw the mountain. He said to his servants, "Stay here with the donkey while I and the boy go over there. We will worship and then we will come back to you" (Genesis 22:5).

This was not an empty assurance. Abraham had been thinking along the way. He had recently come to know Yahweh as the "Eternal God," and to remember that revelation he had planted a tamarisk tree—a hardy bush that appears to live forever (Genesis 21:33). He concluded that since he and Isaac were joined to God, they too would live forever, and he reckoned that God could and would raise his son from the dead (Hebrews 11:19).

So, taking his leave of the servants, the two—father and son—trudged together up the mountain (see Genesis 22:7–8).

"Father?"

"Yes, my son?"

"The fire and wood are here, but where is the lamb?"

"God will provide."

There's such marvelous simplicity in that statement and at the same time such depth. This is the answer to every one of life's dilemmas: "God will provide." Sometimes the simplest things are the profoundest.

The two men finally reached the summit, where Abraham gathered a few rocks and built an altar stone by stone. He laid the fire, bound Isaac, and placed his son—unresisting—on the pyre. Then he lifted his knife . . .

"Abraham! Abraham!"

"Here I am."

"Do not lay a hand on the boy. . . Do not do anything to him. Now I know that you fear God, because you have not withheld from me your son, your only son." Then Abraham saw the ram of God, caught by its horns in a bush, and offered it instead of Isaac. And Abraham called the place Moriah ("The Lord Will Provide"), a memory that became a motto forever. "And to this day it is said, 'On the mountain of the Lord it will be provided'" (Genesis 22:11–14).

What did this ordeal mean to Abraham and God? Only that there was *nothing* between them—no greater love.

Perhaps you're being led up Moriah, being asked to kill some dream, some deep desire. You stare in stark unbelief at the thing God is asking you to do.

It's not so difficult to endure these killings when we see the reason, but when God's will defies logic, when it seems contrary to all that's good for us and others, that's when our love is put to the test.

There's love and logic in all that God does. He knows us well. He sees the things that grip our hearts and tear us away from his love. Like Tolkien's Gollum we have our "Precious"—passions that twine themselves around our hearts and strangle them.

Fenelon wrote, "[God] wants the 'Isaac' of your heart—the only son, the beloved. He wants you to yield up to Him all that you hold most dear. Until you do this you will have no rest. 'Who is he that has resisted the Almighty and been at peace?' Do you want God to bless you? Give up everything to Him and He will be with you. What comfort, what freedom, what strength, what growth when self-love no longer stands between you and God."

Like Abraham we cannot pick the method, the time, or the place of our Moriah. Only God knows; He must choose, and we must let Him. It's easier to bear our losses if we accept them without struggling to escape them. We only make life more difficult for ourselves when we resist God.

Dying is a terribly unique and personal thing. No one can do it for us; it's something that we must do. "Take *your* son," God said to Abraham. But when we give our Isaac—our only hope—to God, He will give us more than we ever hoped for.

It's significant that when Abraham gave his son back to God, God promised again that He would bless all nations through Abraham (Genesis 22:16–19). Now, God said, "You will be fruitful beyond your wildest dreams."

God's gifts are of no value to us or to anyone else until we lose them. When we come to the place that God means more to us than anything else, when we love Him with all our strength and soul and mind and spirit and heart, when we give up the very gift God has given us, then in resurrection power that gift will bring blessing to everyone it touches.

Perhaps God has richly gifted you for ministry but has placed you on the shelf. Remember Abraham and offer up those gifts to God. Face the possibility of never using them again. Be content with the Giver alone. He will provide. He will use you in a new and better way—perhaps in a quieter, hidden way—to enrich many.

Perhaps God has called you to another place. You must give up family, friends, home, and ministry—every comfort zone—and make another place for yourself. This is Moriah. "On the mountain of the Lord it will be provided." Beyond the loneliness and soul-ache lies a new and better life. God will use you to bring righteousness and peace in that place.

This the story of all whose lives have ever counted for God. They have been willing to put to death the very thing they believed was God's gift to them and have contented themselves with God Himself. In so doing He has made them a source of unique and profound blessing to all they know.

This is the paradox of the cross: "Whoever finds his life will lose it, and whoever loses his life for my sake will find it" (Matthew 10:39). "The end of a matter is better than its beginning," the Wise Man said (Ecclesiastes 7:8).

Postscript: Moriah Revisited

About a thousand years after Abraham offered Isaac on Moriah, David bought the entire mountain from Arauvnah, the Canaanite (1 Chronicles 21:25). In David's day Moriah was little more than a scrub-covered, wind-swept hill. Today Jerusalem straddles the mountain.

Moriah is not a single peak but an elongated ridge that begins at the junction of the Kidron and Hinnom Valleys in the south and rises to its peak just northwest of the present Damascus Gate. Jesus was crucified there—on the summit of Mount Moriah.

No one reading about old Abraham, leading his dear son up the mountain, can fail to miss the parallel with God, His own heart breaking, leading His "one and only Son" up Calvary's mountain to the place of the Skull (John 19:17). —

Nothing is said about Isaac's inner struggle, but it must have been intense—a picture for us of Jesus' awful turmoil in the garden of Gethsemane when He faced this very dilemma. God was requiring something that He surely could not be asking. Jesus agonized over that will, sweating, as it were, great drops of blood.

Jesus, like Isaac, was led by His Father to the top of Mount Moriah, bearing the wood of the sacrifice, stumbling under its weight. Jesus, like Isaac, did not open his mouth, but voluntarily was bound to the wood. "He was led like a lamb to the slaughter, and as a sheep before her shearers is silent, so he did not open his mouth" (Isaiah 53:7). Jesus, unlike Isaac, paid the price instead of Isaac and the rest of us. "For the Son of Man did not come to be served, but to serve, and to give his life as a ransom for [instead of] many" (Mark 10:45).

This is the answer to Isaac's question: "Where is the lamb?"—a question asked repeatedly for two thousand years until Jesus came. He is "the Lamb of God, who takes away the sin of the world!" (John 1:29).

This is the answer to Micah's question,

> With what shall I come before the Lord
>   and bow down before the exalted God? . . .
> Shall I offer my firstborn for my transgression,
>   the fruit of my body for the sin of my soul?" (Micah 6:6–7).

No, God does not require our firstborn because He offered up His Son, His *only* Son, the Son whom He *loved* (John 3:16).

Remember the angel's word to Abraham? "Now I know that you fear God, because you have not *withheld* from me your son, your only son" (Genesis 22:12). Using the same Greek word from the Septuagint (the earliest Greek version of the Old Testament) and clearly thinking of this verse, Paul wrote: "He who *did not spare* his own Son, but gave him up for us all—how will he not also, along with him, graciously give us all things?" (Romans 8:32).

God spared Abraham's son; He did not spare His own. Because that is true, will He not give us all things?

—In Quietness and Confidence

A Lesson in Anger Management

The Lord looked with favor on Abel and his offering,
but on Cain and his offering he did not look with favor.
So Cain was very angry, and his face was downcast.
Then the Lord said to Cain, "Why are you angry? Why is your
face downcast? If you do what is right, will you not be accepted?
But if you do not do what is right, sin is crouching at your door;
it desires to have you, but you must master it."
Now Cain said to his brother Abel, "Let's go out to the field." And
while they were in the field, Cain attacked his brother
Abel and killed him.
—Genesis 4:4–8

Anger is a "blanket emotion" that covers an array of other feelings and affections. When our sense of security is imperiled, when we lose power in a relationship, when our imperfections are revealed, when we are rejected, we feel frustrated and angry.

Bottom line, anger is the response we make to outraged love: "The fluid that love bleeds when you cut it," as C. S. Lewis said. What we want is boundless love. When we are frustrated in that pursuit we feel threatened and are propelled into action. We want to fight back.

Threatening situations cause our nervous system to kick in, activating our adrenal glands to secrete chemicals which in turn stimulate a number of organs in our bodies to prepare us to resist and fight. That chemical reaction is what gives us that hard-to-describe feeling of arousal we call anger.

There's nothing sinful about angry feelings. They are an indispensable expression of the natural defense system with which God has equipped us. But when we permit these feelings to push us over the edge, when we give way to blind rage, we demean others, we debase ourselves, and, more important, we dishonor the God in whose image we are created.

We tend to think of anger as an instinctive, reflexive, unconscious, biological reaction beyond our control. Must we then hold ourselves responsible?

We must. The Bible condemns inappropriate expressions of anger and commends those who keep anger under control. The Wise Man said,

> Better a patient man [one slow to anger] than a warrior,
>   a man who controls his temper than one who takes a city (Proverbs 16:32).

> A fool gives full vent to his anger,
>   but a wise man keeps himself under control (Proverbs 29:11).

Recent studies on anger support what the Bible has been saying all along: Anger can be controlled and sanctified through truth. Let me explain.

Anger involves four components: (1) the activating experience (a crying baby, a tardy spouse, a thoughtless remark); (2) an inner emotional reaction to the threat; (3) a series of thoughts that either augment or mitigate the anger; and (4) an outer behavioral response.

These components are so intertwined that we experience them as one continuous surge. That's why we tend to think of anger as an emotion beyond our control. We lose hope for change because we lose sight of the thinking and behaving components of anger and focus on the physiological surge of emotional arousal.

But the behavioral response is governed by our ways of thinking about ourselves and about the person who is making us angry. The intensity of our anger is based on those thoughts. We reach the stage of towering rage because we permit our thoughts to drive us to it.

What I am saying is this: What we think before, during, and after the initial surge of anger determines our outward behavior.

This is nothing new. The Bible makes it clear that any progress toward godliness is the result of proper thinking. Our thought life is the key element in emotional and behavioral control, and that control grows as we acquire additional truth on which to set our minds. We are what we think, Jesus insisted (Matthew 12:35).

James puts all of this together and provides the key: "My dear brothers, take note of this: Everyone should be quick to listen, slow to speak and slow to become angry, for man's anger does not bring about the righteous life that God desires" (1:19–20).

These are the steps James envisions:

1. Acknowledge your anger. It's good to say, "I am getting angry"—to ourselves or to the person with whom we are angry.

It's hard for some people to accept their anger because they falsely equate it with sin, but no emotion is evil in itself. Emotions can only incline us to evil.

2. Hold back your anger. The next step is to be "slow to become angry." In the words of an old slogan, "The only time to procrastinate is when you're angry."

We can and must hold back our anger for a time. This is not repression (holding anger in) but rather a matter of slowing down the rapid escalation of emotion, perhaps by the time-honored expedient of taking a few deep breaths and trying to relax our muscles or counting to ten.

Plutarch, the Roman playwright, had one of his characters say to the emperor, "Remember, Caesar, whenever you are angry, say or do nothing until you have repeated the four-and-twenty letters [of the alphabet] to yourself."

Or, if we feel ourselves getting out of control, we can call time out and separate ourselves temporarily from the conflict or provoking situation, giving our emotions time to subside and allowing our thinking processes time to emerge. A little time out will help us "get our minds right," as Cool Hand Luke would say.

The main thing is to retard our anger and give ourselves time to think. "Anger is the anesthetic of the mind," C. S. Lewis said. Once a certain point is reached, rationality goes out the window. It's important to slow our thought processes down and begin to analyze how we're thinking.

3. Be slow to speak. Literally. Speak slowly or not at all. Restraining our tongues has the effect of slowing down our thought processes, so we can begin to think clearly, rationally, and analytically. Speak when angry, and we inevitably make the best speech we ever regretted.

4. Be quick to listen. And then we should listen—listen to what God has to say and think His thoughts after Him. That's what James means by being "quick to listen." Note the context: "He chose to give us birth through the word of truth, that we might be a kind of firstfruits of all he created. My dear brothers, take note of this: Everyone should be quick to listen, slow to speak and slow to become angry" (1:18–19).

Listen to what? Listen to the "word of truth," an idea he elaborates in verse

22: "Do not merely listen to the word, and so deceive yourselves. Do what it says."

What we must do is slow our thinking down and mentally challenge our thoughts—correct the lies that inform our thoughts and replace them with truth.

All of us have erroneous beliefs about life. We believe against all evidence to the contrary that everything should go our way. Our children should always behave; our opinions should always be considered; our spouses and friends should always be reasonable, cheerful, helpful, and kind; others should always listen to us, understand us, and do our bidding. In short, everyone ought to love us all the time under all conditions of life.

According to psychologist Albert Ellis, the most common mental aberrations are these:

I must always win the approval of others for my performances, or else I am a rotten person.

Others must treat me considerately and kindly and in precisely the way I want them to treat me.

The world (and the people in it) must arrange the conditions under which I live so that I get everything I want when I want it.

That's a pack of lies. We should listen to God's voice and challenge our self-pity, discouragement, and jealousy and replace them with truth:

I live in a broken world with broken people who will frequently break my heart. Nevertheless, I am deeply loved by God.

It's up to God to give me what I need, when He thinks I need it. In the meantime, I am steadfastly kept in His care.

When truth comes in, the lies that have informed our thinking slowly lose their force and our anger begins to abate.

In his treatise *On the Love of God,* Bernard of Clairvaux wrote, "What will you do if your needs are not met? Will you look to God to meet your needs? God promises that those who seek first the kingdom and His righteousness will have all things added to them. God promises that to those who restrict themselves and give to their neighbor He will give whatever is necessary. Seeking first the kingdom means to prefer to bear the yoke of modesty (humility) and restraint rather than allow sin to reign in your mortal body."

Asking God to meet our needs is a better way than our way (and Cain's way) for, as James says, when God meets our needs He gives "more grace" (4:6)—a sense of well-being far greater than anything we can get on our own.

Growth takes time. We must be patient with God while He brings it about. As we learn truth we will develop a mindset that will reduce our emotional reactions to threat. As our hearts become increasingly convinced that God loves us unconditionally and wants to meet our needs, we will find ourselves less inclined to react emotionally to indifference, criticism, or rebuke.

A secure person is less likely to have an adrenaline surge when a client complains about her performance. The person who realizes that God is sovereign and controls all the details of life is less likely to get angry at rush-hour traffic. Men and women who know they are in God's grip can be patient and calm in the face of terror and intimidation.

Of course we will fail. Whoever thought otherwise? But no failure is final. God is a God of an infinite number of chances.

When Leonardo da Vinci was painting *The Last Supper,* he lost his temper at an assistant and lashed the fellow with bitter words. Leonardo returned to his canvas to work on the nearly completed portrait of Jesus, but he could not continue.

Looking into the calm and patient face of Jesus, as he had envisioned Him, Leonardo was reminded of his own tantrum and thoughtless words. Putting down his tools, he sought out the man and asked for forgiveness. Then he went back to his work of making Christ known.

We will fall. As C. S. Lewis pointed out, we will be very dirty children by the time we get home. The only fatal thing is to give up.

—A Man to Match the Mountain

Facing One's Failure

If anybody does sin, we have one who speaks to the Father.
—1 John 2:1

Only a few baseball players have ever batted .400 over an entire season, which means they went hitless six out of ten times. Somehow that makes me feel better about myself.

We focus too much on success stories. Christians, like the champions of Homeric epics, always make it big. I confess I get tired of hearing such heroics. Emerson was right: "Every hero gets to be a bore at last." Personally I'd like to hear a few more stories about failures like me.

Fortunately the Bible is full of them: Noah drank too much. Abraham lied. Moses lost his temper. Gideon lost his nerve. Peter kept putting both feet in his mouth. Paul was sometimes curt and inconsiderate. Mark went home to mother. Thomas doubted. Most biblical men and women cut unheroic figures, but they're still my heroes. I need some failures to look up to now and then.

David is my favorite—he muffed it so many times. And yet the Bible described him as a man after God's own heart. How can it be? Is there hope for a sinner like me? It seems there is; it all depends on the state of the heart.

David is best known for his affair with Uriah's wife, Bathsheba, whom he saw exposed on her patio. One wrong thing led to another. As Augustine would say, "Her caresses drew his spirit down." Bathsheba got pregnant. David put out a contract on her husband Uriah, an old friend, and after Uriah's death, David married Bathsheba to put a legal and final end to the sordid affair.

Or so he thought.

The law of inevitable consequence caught up with the king. He had to face the facts; or, more precisely, he had to face Nathan, who dug up the facts. The prophet trapped David with a trumped-up story about a rich man who stole another man's lamb to serve a "traveling stranger," Nathan's metaphor for David's transient passion.

When David heard the story he was outraged. "As surely as the Lord lives, the man who did this deserves to die!" David, of course, overreacted; sheep nabbing was not a capital crime. Or perhaps he knew what Nathan was really talking about. When David realized that Nathan had his number, his defenses crumbled. "I have sinned against the Lord," he said (2 Samuel 12:13). David didn't cover up; he faced his failure and repented of it, and the Lord took away his sin. David bore the serious consequences of his sin, but his walk with God resumed. He could go on.

Some of David's most poignant and powerful poems were composed during this period (Psalms 32, 38, 51). They reveal the state of his heart.

> I acknowledged my sin to you
>   and did not cover up my iniquity.
> I said, "I will confess
>   my transgressions to the Lord"—
> and you forgave
>   the guilt of my sin.
> Therefore let everyone who is godly pray to you
>   while you may be found (Psalm 32:5–6).

The word *godly* may put us off because we may think of someone who is sinless. The original word merely signified one who was loyal to the Lord and longed to please Him.

Anyone can be godly because what matters most is not performance but the inclination of the heart. As Jesus said,

> Blessed are those who hunger and thirst for righteousness,
>   for they will be filled (Matthew 5:6).

God doesn't look for perfection. He knows the miserable stuff of which we're made. The godly will surely sin, and just as certainly their sins will be found out. God reveals our waywardness to heal us. We will notice defilement because He will show it to us. Such work in us is the sign of His presence.

When that sin is faced and repented of, it is forgiven. Then we can go on. And going on, after all, is what matters. God doesn't require perfection, only progress.

C. S. Lewis wrote, "No amount of falls will really undo us if we keep picking ourselves up each time."

—The Strength of a Man

Character Counts

Forgive my hidden faults.
Keep your servant also from [these] willful sins;
* may they not rule over me.*
Then I will be blameless,
* innocent of great transgression.*
May the words of my mouth and the meditation of my heart
* be pleasing in your sight,*
* O Lord, my Rock and my Redeemer.*
                    —Psalm 19:12–14

I was fishing Lick Creek one day and cast my fly into a willow. It was the last fly of that pattern and the only one that was working. I said a very bad word. There are some things bad enough to make a preacher cuss, but my reaction surprised me. I hadn't used that word for a while. I wondered where it came from. But I was safe. Carolyn was fishing one hundred yards or so downstream, and we were more than one hundred miles from my parish and twenty miles from the nearest town. There was no one around to hear.

Late that evening while I was attempting to set up the trailer, one piece of equipment would not work right. It was a warm, humid night, and soon I was wringing wet and utterly frustrated. Carolyn tried to be helpful, offering advice since she couldn't offer anything else at the time.

I got annoyed and suggested that if she should like to try to start my car I would sit in hers and blow the horn. It's an old joke that she didn't find funny. Nor did I—I followed up with some angry words. Again, it surprised me. I rarely talked to her that way. But mostly I was chagrined because there was someone around to hear. I looked up from under the trailer into the eyes of two nearby kayakers who were taking in the whole scene. But once more I was safe—they were from California.

As Carolyn and I talked about the two incidents the next morning on the way back to Boise, I realized afresh that what I was in private was the real me. I had kidded myself into believing that my public image was what I was, but that was my illusion. The way I behave when there's no one around to hear or see is *me!* Everything else is a sham.

Dickens wrote about telescopic philanthropy—compassion for those at a distance but not for those at hand. I've always applied that principle to others, to those who decry apartheid but act as shamelessly as a South African bureaucrat toward those of other races in the United States. I don't apply the truth to myself. As Tolstoy said, "Everybody thinks of changing humanity and nobody thinks of changing himself."

I can talk about compassion for others and yet be utterly tactless and inconsiderate to my own family. In which case, what I am at home is what I am. Or I can think myself reasoned and self-controlled, but what I do and say when angry and unobserved gives me away. My character is what I am when I'm alone.

I have a mountain friend who winters in a backcountry ranch all alone. He doesn't have a radio and doesn't read much. Most of the time he's snowed in. I asked him once what he did while he was there by himself. "Well," he mused, "I get to know myself real good." That sounded like wisdom then, and it still does. If I would know myself well, I must know myself when I'm alone.

There's old Adam within, with vast potential for greed and selfishness. I know I can't change him much. Frontal attack has never worked for me. As soon as I resist sin, I endow it with more power. This same power it uses against me. Inner transformation, thus, is God's work. As Mother Teresa put it, we may *will* holiness, but He must do it.

What's needed is more of God in me. He must work His work. Righteousness is His gift, which I may receive. David's prayer in Psalm 19:12–14 becomes my own.

—The Strength of a Man

God Discerns the Possibilities

*Then Ziba said to the king, "Your servant will do whatever my
lord the king commands his servant to do."*
—2 Samuel 9:11

Jonathan, the son of King Saul, had a son whose name was Meribaal. He
was five years old when news of Jonathan's death came from Gilboa. His
nurse, expecting the Philistines to overrun the citadel, snatched up the child
and fled, but in her panic she fell and the child was severely injured. As a result, he "became crippled," the beginning of a tortured, melancholy life. His
humiliation was so deep that his name was changed from Meribaal ("The
Lord Is My Advocate") to Mephibosheth (*Mephi* means something like "My
Brokenness" and *bosheth* means "Shame").

"We shouldn't take names to ourselves," Tolkien's Frodo said to the
self-pitying creature Sméagol. "It's unwise whether true or false." But
Mephibosheth couldn't avoid the name change. He thought of himself as a
ruined man, and in all his utterances he speaks as a weary, dispirited soul.

Some years later David recalled an oath he had sworn to Jonathan: "Show
me unfailing kindness like that of the Lord as long as I live . . . and do not
ever cut off your kindness from my family . . . And Jonathan had David reaf-
firm his oath out of love for him" (1 Samuel 20:14–15, 17).

David determined to keep his word to his dear friend, so he asked Saul's
old servant, Ziba, if any of Jonathan's descendants still lived. "Oh, yes," Ziba
replied. "One of Jonathan's sons is still alive, but he's crippled in both feet."

David immediately had Mephibosheth brought to him from exile
(Mephibosheth was living across the Jordan, far from the family estate and
David's court) and welcomed him into his presence.

"Mephibosheth!" the king cried with joy when he saw the son of his old friend.

"Your servant," Mephibosheth replied as he fell to his knees, thinking that David would surely kill him. (It was the custom in other cultures then to kill all presumptive heirs to the throne.)

But David said, "Don't be afraid, Mephibosheth. You will eat at my table for the rest of your life."

We see our story in Mephibosheth's. As David himself put it, this is "the love of the Lord." (The word *kindness* in 2 Samuel 9:7 is "covenant love," the love God has for us.) God does not say, "Learn to walk well, and I'll take you in." He loves us as David loved Mephibosheth—*as is.* We stagger and falter, we stumble and fall; yet He receives us and invites us to eat at His table.

Our decision to come to Him may be nothing more than the desperate culmination of a lifetime of failure. We may have struggled so long with our fallen and failed nature that we've given up. But God does not despair of us even when we've despaired of ourselves. "He is eternal," Augustine said, "therefore His love endures forever."

Some of us are so broken that our personalities resist change. Yet God discerns the possibilities in the most damaged life. He can take all that's unworthy in it and, as it pleases Him, gradually turn it into good, though for reasons known only to God, some of us may glorify Him for a time through our brokenness. Some of us are so handicapped that complete healing awaits heaven's cure. Yet we can be assured today of God's everlasting favor and love.

Mephibosheth "*always* ate at the king's table, [though] he was crippled in both feet," the narrator concludes (9:13). Mephibosheth never walked as a man should walk, but he always had a place at the king's table.

And the tablecloth covered his feet.[3]

—Out of the Ordinary

---

3. I am indebted to Dr. Howard Hendricks for this phrase.

Facing Our Fears

After this, the Moabites and Ammonites with some of the Meunites
came to make war on Jehoshaphat.
Some men came and told Jehoshaphat, "A vast army is coming
against you from Edom, from the other side of the Sea. It is
already in Hazazon Tamar" . . . Alarmed, Jehoshaphat resolved
to inquire of the Lord, and he proclaimed a fast for all Judah. The
people of Judah came together to seek help from the Lord; indeed,
they came from every town in Judah to seek him.
—2 Chronicles 20:1–4

Marine Corps Lieutenant General Chesty Puller once referred to the Korean Conflict as a "dirty little war, but the only one we have." I was in the military then, and though I never saw combat in Korea, I saw some of the casualties. It was an engagement in which the enemy refused to fight fair.

I've seen the look of terror in men's eyes, unfaded by years of relative safety—the look of men who've been to hell and back and can't forget what they've seen.

I've seen that same terrible look in the eyes of men who've told me they have prostate cancer, are victims of corporate downsizing, are facing bankruptcy and ruin, or have been abandoned by their wives. They too look as though they've been to hell and back; they too have seen an enemy that will not fight fair.

There is an irony about anxiety, however, that takes away its power. It can make us braver than we ever were before. Courage is not fearlessness, but a settled disposition to do what is right in the face of our fear. "Courage is not the absence of fear," reads a line in *The Red Badge of Courage,* "it is the ability to do what we must."

There's a narrative in the Old Testament that makes that point. It's the story of King Jehoshaphat, a man who learned to face down his fears.

Jehoshaphat was a relatively obscure ruler of the southern kingdom of Judah. Second Chronicles 20 reports on a day "after this" that began like any other day, but quickly turned into chaos.

It is significant that these armies from the east massed and mounted their attack at this particular time. Jehoshaphat was on a high. This was a time of great victory for the young king. God had made him His instrument to bring about a great revival (2 Chronicles 19:4–11).

With the announcement of the invasion, King Jehoshaphat came down from his high in a hurry. Hazazon Tamar was only fifteen miles from Jerusalem, less than a day's march away.

This was a daring and unexpected move in which the invaders crossed the Dead Sea, probably at a ford opposite Masada, and climbed one of the difficult assents directly into the heart of the Judean hills. Before Jehoshaphat was aware of their presence, they were in position to strike Jerusalem, the capital city of Judah. The crisis was total!

Jehoshaphat was badly frightened, and he admitted it—unlike some men who deny their fear. It's too bad that they do, because the first step to overcoming any anxiety is to face it.

Fear ought to lead us to do the best thing, what Jehoshaphat did. He inquired of the Lord and sought help from Him. Jehoshaphat, an extraordinary man, stood with his people in the house of the Lord and prayed (20:5–13).

Jehoshaphat focused first on God and found that everything was under control in heaven and earth. At ground level the view was appalling, but there was no panic above. "God works in tranquillity," one old saint has said. And those who know the God of peace share His calm and quiet nature.

Then Jehoshaphat looked back and thought about God's faithfulness in the past: "O our God, did you not drive out the inhabitants of this land before your people Israel and give it forever to the descendants of Abraham, your friend?" (20:7).

He reminded himself that God had given Canaan to His people by covenant; He had guaranteed their integrity in the land. No one could oust them without His permission.

Those who had lived when God gave Israel land and had learned their faith back then said that when crises came, a man could cry out to God in his distress, and he would be heard and saved (20:9). And so Jehoshaphat prayed, "Now here are men from Ammon, Moab and Mount Seir . . . O our God will you not judge them? For we have no power to face this vast army that is attacking us. We do not know what to do, but our eyes are on you" (20:10–12).

There is a significant juxtaposition of two thoughts here: "Power and might are in your hand" (20:6), and "We have no power" (20:12).

We have no power; God has it all. He does not give power to anyone in the sense that His power is ours to have and to hold. We are always weak. We are never strong. The only strength we have is the strength that comes from God. "Not that we are competent in ourselves," Paul echoes, "but our competence comes from God" (2 Corinthians 3:5).

Sometimes we feel weak; sometimes we feel strong. But we must always keep in mind that we are never strong, even when we feel that way. We are always needy, always incompetent, always inadequate, always inept, always desperately dependent on God. Without Him we can do nothing.

Perhaps the most startling of all Jesus' statements about Himself was His insistence that He too was an inadequate being. "By myself," He said, "I can do nothing" (John 5:30).

Jesus' incarnation included taking on our weakness. He, like us, had to rely on God every moment of every day. Each morning He had to abandon His own strength and strategies and offer Himself up, confident that His Father's power would lead Him into greater works than He could envision or accomplish alone. "Oh the mystery of humility," F. B. Meyer said, "that He who planned all things should live a life of such absolute dependence."

I recall walking into Ray Stedman's office one day to lament my own limitations. Some months before, I had been handed a large ministry. I knew I would surely fail. "I'm so inadequate," I bemoaned.

"Yes, you are, my friend—and so am I," Ray quipped, "and it's good that we know it. Some men labor all their lives never knowing that they're inadequate."

Jehoshaphat knew. He looked at his limitations and then looked to the Lord as the only source of his help: "We do not know what to do, but our eyes are upon you." That's a prayer we should breathe every moment of every day, not just when our backs are against the wall. When that becomes our mindset, significant things begin to happen.

G. K. Chesterton pointed out that if a man needs wisdom, he may cry out, "William Shakespeare, help me!" and nothing much will happen. If he needs courage, he may cry out, "Billy Budd, help me!" and nothing much will happen. But for two thousand years, whenever a man has cried out, "Lord Jesus, help me," something momentous has happened.

Something happened after Jehoshaphat's plea. Someone in the crowd spoke up—Jahaziel, one of the brothers:

> Listen, King Jehoshaphat and all who live in Judah and Jerusalem! This is what the Lord says to you: "Do not be afraid or discouraged because of this vast army. For the battle is not yours, but God's. Tomorrow march down against them . . . You will not have to fight this battle. Take up your positions; stand firm and see the deliverance the Lord will give you . . . Do not be afraid; do not be discouraged. Go out to face them tomorrow, and the Lord will be with you" (2 Chronicles 20:15–17).

The battle was the Lord's. It was His business to do the fighting. Jehoshaphat's role was to stand fast and see what God would do. This is what Paul meant when he wrote, "Be strong in the Lord and in his mighty power. Put on the full armor of God so that you can take your stand against the devil's schemes . . . Therefore put on the full armor of God, so that when the day of evil comes, you may be able to stand your ground, and after you have done everything, to stand" (Ephesians 6:10–13).

"Standing" is a mental posture, a refusal to run away, to retreat into self-indulgent and self-protective devices. It is a matter of standing one's ground and waiting to see what God will do.

But standing also means engaging our fears. We have to "march down against them"; we must identify the thing we fear and face it. That's sometimes the hardest thing in the world to do. Our natural inclination is to flee.

We must not run from our fears; we only expose ourselves to greater danger when we do. We must "get in the face" of those things we fear and then see what God will do.

The next morning Jehoshaphat's fears returned, as they always do, but he looked again into God's Word and found there the assurance he needed to go on. He said to his army, "Have faith in the Lord your God and you will be upheld; have faith in his prophets and you will be successful" (2 Chronicles 20:20). Faith comes by hearing and hearing by the Word of God.

Again, we see this in Paul's writing: "Take up the shield of faith, with which you can extinguish all the flaming arrows of the evil one. Take the helmet of salvation and the sword of the Spirit, which is the word of God" (Ephesians 6:16–17).

Satan never gives up. He continues to harass us, reminding us of our impotence and inability to act, insinuating that God cannot be trusted to keep His word. "Has God really said . . . ?" he sneers.

He flings himself against us again and again. He tries to overwhelm us with repeated assaults. For each attack we must raise the shield of faith and unsheathe our swords—stir ourselves to remember what God has said and get a good grip on His Word.

So then, with confidence restored, Jehoshaphat marched off to face his foes. The band struck up a tune, and Jehoshaphat and his army went off to war, singing an old sustaining song:

> Give thanks to the Lord,
>   for his love endures forever (2 Chronicles 20:21).

Imagine the march. Jehoshaphat reached the top of the first hill from which he could look down into the Jordan valley. There he saw his enemies massing for the attack. Then they were lost from sight as he dropped into a valley.

He climbed another hill from which he could look down and see the enemy on the march up the wadi. He descended and once again his enemies disappeared from view only to appear again at the next rise. Each hill became another occasion to renew his faith.

Then as he approached the final hilltop, he drew his sword and led the charge—to find "only dead bodies lying on the ground" (20:24). "The Lord set ambushes against the men of Ammon and Moab and Mount Seir who were invading Judah, and they were defeated. The men of Ammon and Moab rose up against the men from Mount Seir to destroy and annihilate them. After they finished slaughtering the men from Seir, they helped to destroy one another" (20:22–23). Jehoshaphat's enemies were DOA. There was nothing left of them but their booty.

There's an old saying: "To a crow in the know a scarecrow is an invitation to a feast." Jehoshaphat and his army plundered their adversaries and returned with the spoils of war. Is this not what Paul means when he says we are "more than conquerors through him who loved us" (Romans 8:37)? God takes the very thing we fear and turns it to ringing triumph.

This assault upon Judah is suggestive to me of those unexpected crises we experience that come out of nowhere, often at a time when things are going especially well.

When we least expect it, a messenger arrives at our house with a registered letter from a lawyer; a summons comes from the IRS; a warrant is served for our son's arrest; our doctor leaves a call informing us that our lab tests look bad. The fear we experience at such times is perfectly normal. It is not cowardice. It is a natural, instinctive reaction to a situation beyond our control.

I'm personally afraid of men who are fearless. Starbuck, the chief mate of Captain Ahab's boat *The Pequod,* said, "I will have no man in my boat who is not afraid of a whale." I agree. I don't drift our Idaho rivers with men who have no fear, and I don't fly with bush pilots who aren't afraid. There are old pilots and bold pilots, as they say, but there are no old, bold pilots. There are some things a man ought to be afraid of. If he isn't, there's something wrong with him.

The problem is not fear, but our response to it. Jesus often said to His disciples, "fear not," but the tense He employed referred not to their immediate response to danger, but to *persistent* fear—fear that paralyzes and hinders them from doing what they knew they ought to do.

Though I rarely agree with theologian Paul Tillich, I think he had the right idea when he argued that courage is the foundation of virtue. Fear is what prevents obedience.

Fear is not sin, but disobedience is, and fear can lead to disobedience. We listen to our racing pulses and ringing ears and react in ungodly ways. We lash out at our colleagues, our wife and children, and God. We deny our fear and cover up with bravado or we flee from it into alcohol and drugs. We resort to scheming on our own and make decisions that exclude God's wisdom. As a consequence we never find out what God can do.

We should rather seek God's face and that tranquil place where He dwells. There's no panic there. In that quiet place we must read and reflect on His Word and find out what He wants us to do. He will supply the wisdom we need.

And then we must sally forth in faith to face the thing we fear, singing to ourselves about our Lord's love, thanking Him for a victory already won, believing that the battle is not ours but the Lord's.

He will do all the rest. He will either do away with our enemies, or He will take us through the encounter unscathed. He will deliver us from evil and surprise us with joy. The valley we have dreaded will have become a valley of blessing forevermore (2 Chronicles 20:26).

The prophet Joel, when speaking about the coming of our Lord, calls the place of His final conflict "the Valley of Jehoshaphat" (Joel 3:2, 12). Jehoshaphat's victory in his day was symbolic of all God's victories and finds its final application in the ultimate defeat of all the enemies of our soul.

In the meantime, every dark and dangerous valley can be the Valley of Jehoshaphat—the place where God puts to death our fears.

—*A Man to Match the Mountain*

If I Were a Rich Man

The brother in humble circumstances ought to take pride in his high position. But the one who is rich should take pride in his low position, because he will pass away like a wild flower. For the sun rises with scorching heat and withers the plant; its blossom falls and its beauty is destroyed. In the same way, the rich man will fade away even while he goes about his business.
—James 1:9–11

We spoil our entire lives trying to accumulate money. We ruin our vacations, health, marriages, children, and friendships—and for what? In the end we wither and die and leave our wealth behind. That's why money, no matter how much we have, is a bad investment.

There's more to money, however, than the fact that we leave it behind. The greater problem is that it can ruin our lives right *now*. It makes us believe that money, when we have enough of it, will make us secure and significant.

In the introduction to his book *Money and the Meaning of Life*, Jacob Needleman wrote, "I have always pictured poverty as associated with fear and anxiety about the future, fear of abandonment, fear of physical danger, and fear of loneliness. I see the poor as trapped, tense, cunning, harsh. I see them bored, empty of hope, or consumed by absurd fantasies." The answer, he continued, is to make money, for money talks and tells us we're very significant.

Money does talk, but mostly it lies to us. It really isn't true that money will make us feel successful and secure. The well-heeled *know* it isn't true. Enough is never enough. Having money is just a goad to get more.

Furthermore, money also deceives us by telling us we're wise and powerful. As Tevya, the fiddler on the roof, mused, when you're rich it doesn't matter if you answer right or wrong, " 'cause when you're rich they think you really know." But isn't it odd that rich men, stripped of their wealth, are often considered great fools?

Financial ruin can make you look foolish, but it can also be an occasion to gain great wisdom. It teaches us James' odd inversion: "The brother in humble circumstances ought to take pride in his *high* position. But the one who is rich should take pride in his *low* position" (James 1:9–10).

Poverty can enrich us because in it we learn the secret of true wealth. Being rich isn't about money, you see; it's a state of mind. There is a wealth that leaves us poverty-stricken and a poverty that makes us fabulously rich.

Money, if we love it, will impoverish us, for it will turn our hearts from good. "If your eyes are bad," Jesus said, "your whole body will be full of darkness. If then the light within you is darkness, how great is that darkness!" (Matthew 6:23).

If we fix our eyes on mammon [material wealth], it will darken our hearts, cloud our judgment, and leave us morally confused and uncertain. It will lead us into bad decisions—choices that defy logic and cause us to deny our highest values. We will fudge, cheat, embezzle, misappropriate, pad, and pilfer. We will, in the end, do anything to make a buck. The light in our hearts will go out and, as Jesus said, "How great is that darkness!" (Matthew 6:23).

But worse, the love of money will turn our hearts from God. "No one can serve two masters," Jesus said. "Either he will hate the one and love the other, or he will be devoted to the one and despise the other. You cannot serve both God and Money" (Matthew 6:24). If we think about money all the time, we will, in time, take no thought of God. Wanting money—what wise men call *greed*—is a state of mind in which it's easier to forget God than any other.

John Bunyan, in *The Pilgrim's Progress*, described the ruin of some travelers: "Now on the far side of that plain was a little hill called Lucre and in that hill [there was] a silver mine, which some of them, because of the rarity of it, had turned aside to see. But going too near the brim of the pit the ground being deceitful under them broke and they were slain. Some also had been maimed there, and could not to their dying day be their own men again."

If we love money, that devotion will inexorably supplant our passion for God, and we will be maimed and slain by it. We will be "devoted to the one" and will "despise the other." We may dabble with God for a time, but in the end we will deny Him. "One master-passion in the breast. . . swallows up the rest," said Alexander Pope.

So God in His mercy will do one of two things for us: He will give us money and leave us with heart-breaking disappointment in it, or He will take it all away. Either way, God is at work, humbling us, ridding us of our preoccupation with mammon, loosening our grip on "earth's toys and lesser joys," as my wife Carolyn says, setting our affection on things above. This is the ruin that enriches us, the "low position" that leaves us better than ever before.

What God leaves behind is pure gold: We have God and all that He gives. We need nothing more. Israel's poet wrote out of his poverty:

> I am always with you;
> > you hold me by my right hand.
> You guide me with your counsel,
> > and afterward you will take me into glory.
> Whom have I in heaven but you?
> > And earth has nothing I desire besides you . . .
> As for me, it is good to be near God (Psalm 73:23–25, 28).

This is the good life. This is the richest man on earth!

—Growing Slowly Wise

Developing the Quieter Virtues

*Whether the cloud stayed over the tabernacle for two days or a
month or a year, the Israelites would remain in camp and not set
out; but when it lifted, they would set out.*
—Numbers 9:22

I watch the thunderheads mass and billow over the Boise Front and think of "the cloud"—the symbol of the Presence in Israel's midst and the means by which God's people were led through the wilderness.

Moses had this to say about the cloud: "Sometimes the cloud was over the tabernacle only a few days" (Numbers 9:20); other times the cloud "remained over the tabernacle a long time" (9:19)—several days, a month, a year—and God's people waited and waited and waited . . .

Waiting is hard. We twiddle our thumbs, shuffle our feet, stifle our yawns, and fret inwardly in frustration. We want to hit the road.

"Ah, for the open road," sighs Mr. Toad in *The Wind in the Willows.* "There's the real life for you . . . Here today and off somewhere else tomorrow! Travel, change, interest, excitement! The whole world before you, and a horizon that's always changing."

Like Toady, we want to put miles behind us, see new sights. Change, interest, excitement! That's the life! But the cloud lingers, and so do we. We feel trapped by drab routine; day-in and day-out duty; the monotonous grind; the same ol', same ol'.

We writhe under our frustration and helplessness. "This is no place to grow," we complain. "What chance do I have to develop my full potential? What opportunity do I have to accomplish great things?" "Haven't I endured enough?" we ask. "Haven't I learned the lesson of this place?" "Isn't it time to move on?"

"No," is often the answer. The cloud lingers, and we make no progress at all—or so it seems to us.

But what seems so is not what is so. Waiting is not an interruption of our journey but an essential part of it. Without delay we could never make the most of our lives. It's one of the ways God affects the ends on which He has set His heart.

Waiting is the time for soul making, the time to develop the quieter virtues—submission, humility, patience, endurance, persistence. The quiet virtues take the longest to learn, are the last to be learned, and, it seems, can be learned only through God's delays, the very thing we're most inclined to resist.

We mustn't resist, and we mustn't grow restless. We must wait before we make a change by some rash and willful act—before we give notice to a difficult employer, before we walk out on a hard marriage, before we trash a disappointing friendship, or make some other irrevocable decision. We must wait to make the next move. We'll know when it's time to go. God will make the change in plenty of time.

In the meantime we should look into each delay for its disciplines, learning its deeper lessons of faith and obedience and yielding to God's efforts to change *us* rather than our circumstances. The extent to which we do so will determine the extent to which His purposes are achieved in us or are thwarted.

F. B. Meyer said, "What a chapter might be written of God's delays. It is the mystery of educating human spirits to the finest temper of which they are capable. What searchings of the heart, what analyzings of motives, what testings of the Word of God, what upliftings of the soul . . . All these are associated with these weary days of waiting which are, nevertheless, big with spiritual destiny."

—In Quietness and Confidence

Take Your Burdens to the Lord

This is what the Lord says: "Be careful not to carry a load on the Sabbath day or bring it through the gates of Jerusalem. Do not bring a load out of your houses or do any work on the Sabbath."
—Jeremiah 17:21–22

Never underestimate the value of . . . not bothering.
—Winnie the Pooh

Not bothering"—I like Pooh's advice. Would that I, like that wise old bear, could lead a less bothered life.

Jeremiah speaks to that tendency to bother oneself with life's burdens: "Be careful not to carry a load on the Sabbath," he said. It's an odd text to fix on, but it sets my mind right. Let me explain.

To proclaim his message, Jeremiah took his stand in the city gates of Jerusalem, where all who walked by could hear him.

It's odd that Jeremiah would stress Sabbath observance when so much was wrong with the city, but it was essential to do so because the Sabbath is at the heart of what ails us—our tendency to work ourselves to death when God wants to give us rest.

Rest is the oldest institution in the world. It was established in the beginning when God set out to make the world. He worked six days, we're told, and then took a day off. Then God wrote that day large in Israel's law book and on her calendar. He called the day *Sabbath,* a word that means "to cease from one's labors, to rest."

It was Augustine who first noted that the phrase "there was evening, and there was morning," which occurs on each of the first six days of creation, is conspicuously absent on the seventh day. The seventh day had a beginning, but it had no end. God's rest goes on forever.

This restful seventh day was a symbolic rule for Israel, but for us now it's a daily reality—that "spiritual rest, in which believers lay aside their own works to allow God to work for them," as John Calvin said. The Sabbath was once a day to rest; now it's an everyday thing (Colossians 2:16–17; Hebrews 4:1–11).

The Sabbath is not a day, it's a disposition—a mindset of resting every day, all day, for all we have to accomplish, believing that God is at the heart of all our activity. It's an unencumbered, unhurried, relaxed lifestyle that grows out of a deep awareness that God is on the job twenty-four hours a day whether we are or not.

Solomon wrote,

> In vain you rise early
> and stay up late,
> toiling for food to eat—
> for [God] grants sleep to those he loves (Psalm 127:2).

There's something wonderfully significant about this psalm, something easily missed unless we understand that the Sabbath for Israel began not on Saturday morning but on Friday evening at bedtime.

The Hebrew evening and morning sequence says something significant to us: God puts His children to sleep so He can get his work done. "Sleep is God's contrivance for giving us the help he cannot get into us when we are awake," said George MacDonald.

In the evening fatigue overtakes us, and we have to stop working. We lay ourselves down to sleep and drift off into blessed oblivion for the next six to eight hours, a state in which we are totally nonproductive. But nothing essential stops. Though we may leave many things undone, many projects unfinished, God is still at work. "He grants sleep to those he loves." The next morning His eyes sweep over us, and He awakens us to enjoy the benefits of all that He has done.

Most of us, however, hit the floor running. We wolf down a Power Bar and dash out the door with a travel mug of coffee clutched in our hand. We have to be up and doing, getting things started and getting a world of things done. That's because we don't yet understand that God has been working for us all along. We have awakened into a world in which everything was started centuries ago. God has been preparing the good works in which we find ourselves walking each day (Ephesians 2:10).

F. B. Meyer said, "We must remember to maintain within our hearts the spirit of Sabbath calm and peace, not fussy, not anxious, nor fretful nor impetuous; refraining our feet from our own paths, our hand from our own devices, refusing to make our own joy and do our own works. It is only when we are fully resolved to act thus, allowing God to originate His own plans and to work in us for their accomplishment that we enter into rest."

And what keeps us from entering into God's rest? Unbelief. Underlying all our worry and compulsive self-effort is the thought that God cannot or will not come through. That's why the people of Israel wouldn't lay their burdens down in Jeremiah's day, and that's why we can't let up. That's why we have to keep hustling and hoping to do more. That's why we get so weary and worn out. That's why we get so worried. And that's why we need to find rest.

Can we do it? You bet your life we can. We can keep the Sabbath inwardly and carry no burdens through the gates of our minds. The necessary is always possible. God never commands without giving us the means to comply.

Here's what we must do: We must greet anxiety at the door with one short, strong answer—"God." We must say to ourselves, as Abraham said to Isaac in his moment of greatest worry, "God will provide" (Genesis 22:8). And then we must leave the matter with Him. That's how we enter into His rest.

Paul said the same thing: "Do not be anxious about anything, but in everything, by prayer and petition, with thanksgiving, present your requests to God. And the peace of God, which transcends all understanding, will guard your hearts and your minds in Christ Jesus" (Philippians 4:6–7).

Our wills can direct our thoughts to any object they choose. We can either obsess over our fear or look away from it and direct our thoughts toward God and His perfect solutions. It's good to think objectively about the issues that distress us, but to fret over them is to deny God's love for us and His ability to save.

Years ago I was walking a streambed with my brother-in-law, Ed Wichern, accompanied by his son David, who was about three years old. David was collecting "piglets," as he called them, round stream rocks that did indeed look like Winnie the Pooh's porcine friend.

The accumulation of rocks soon got to be too much for David, who struggled along unable to keep up. "Let me carry your piglets, David," Ed said. "No," David replied firmly. "You carry me, and I'll carry my piglets."

I couldn't help but think then, and many times since then, how David's childish self-reliance rebukes my own grown-up reluctance to let God take my burdens. "You carry me," I insist, "but all the cares of life are my own." Much better, Peter insisted, to cast all our anxiety on Him because He cares about us (1 Peter 5:7).

—In Quietness and Confidence

of all earth's diseases, leprosy is
the only one singled out and linked
with sin. It was a dirty disease
that rendered its victim "unclean"
"Sin come to the surface"
Lepers were cut off from the land
of the living.

We Must Come Down

Naaman's servants went to him and said, "My father, if the prophet had told you to do some great thing, would you not have done it? How much more, then, when he tells you, 'Wash and be cleansed'!" So he went down and dipped himself in the Jordan seven times, as the man of God had told him, and his flesh was restored and became clean like that of a young boy.
—2 Kings 5:13–14

Rabbinic tradition holds that Naaman was the anonymous soldier at the battle of Ramoth Gilead whose "random" shot mortally wounded Ahab, the king of Israel (1 Kings 22:34), and for that reason Syria's victory was attributed to him (2 Kings 5:1). He rose through the ranks to become commander of the army.

Naaman had honor, celebrity, and power, but he was a leper—all lesions and stumps, discolored and deformed, corrupted, shocking in his ugliness, a gross, grisly caricature of what a man was intended to be. Leprosy is one of the most appalling diseases known to humankind. It is treatable today, but in Naaman's day it was terminal. Odd, isn't it, how a little bacillus can bring a big man down?

Of all earth's diseases, leprosy is the only one singled out and linked with sin. It was a "dirty" disease that rendered its victims "unclean," a word that suggests the antithesis of holy.

It's not that leprosy itself was sinful; the disease was rather a metaphor for sin—sin come to the surface. If one could see the fetid, disgusting sight of it, sin would look like an advanced case of leprosy. And, like sin, the end of leprosy is death: Lepers were "cut off from the land of the living" and required to wear clothing emblematic of perpetual mourning for the dead (Leviticus 13:45–46). So with sin: We are stone-cold dead in trespasses and sin; "myself, my sepulcher, a moving grave," as John Milton described it.

God had a solution for Naaman's living death. It began with the loving concern of a little girl. We don't know her name. She was just a slave, taken captive from the land of Israel.

The story is necessarily concise; nothing is said about the terror of her abduction, the separation from her family, or the crushing grief of her parents. Nor is there any hint in her of that bitter rage against an adversary that goes by the name of holy zeal. She saw her servitude as an opportunity to serve God in some way. Her occasion came with the serious illness of her master.

Instead of thinking of his disease as justice, she sought help for him, the only help that anyone can give: She wanted to bring him to the living God, where he could find "help . . . in our time of need" (Hebrews 4:16).

She said to her mistress, "If only my master would see the prophet who is in Samaria! He would cure him of his leprosy" (2 Kings 5:3). The rabbis call attention to the peculiar construction of the sentence and render it, "If only the *supplications* (prayers) of my master could be set before the prophet who is in Samaria." Naaman was a hard man, but underneath there was quiet desperation. He was dying, and there was nothing anyone could do.

Naaman's wife reported the conversation to him, who in turn sought permission from the king to visit Samaria, the capital of Israel. He needed permission and letters of safe conduct, because Israel and Syria were not on friendly terms. The king sent him off with a military escort and a letter to Joram, king of Israel, that said in part, "With this letter I am sending my servant Naaman to you so that you may cure him of his leprosy" (5:6).

The intent of the letter was to get Naaman in touch with Elisha, as oriental kings were then in close contact with their prophets and priests. The king of Syria assumed that this was the case in Israel and that Joram would simply hand the case over to his prophet.

But Joram had no use for God and His prophet and assumed that everything depended on him. He read the letter, tore his robes, and wailed, "Am I God? Can I kill and bring back to life? Why does this fellow send someone to me to be cured of his leprosy? See how he is trying to pick a quarrel with me!" (5:7).

Ben-Hadad, the king of Syria, took the girl's words seriously. Joram didn't. The king of Israel, who had the wisdom of the prophets at hand, knew more and believed less than his pagan counterpart.

The King of Israel believed less than his PAGAN counterpart

Somehow Elisha got wind of the matter and sent word to Joram: "Have the man come to me and he will know there is a prophet in Israel" (5:8). So the great Naaman went with his entourage and summoned the prophet to appear.

Naaman thought the prophet would come out of his house and put on a show—prance and dance, wave his hands over him, shout abracadabra, or make some other hocus-pocus. After all, Naaman was an important man. (The verb translated "surely come" indicates that he thought that Elisha, whom he regarded as his social inferior, had an obligation to come out to meet him. Furthermore, "to me" is in an emphatic position in the sentence, suggesting "to someone as important as I!")

But Elisha did not come out to greet Naaman. He simply announced God's word: "Go, wash yourself seven times in the Jordan, and your flesh will be restored and you will be cleansed" (5:10).

Here is double indignity: Elisha not only failed to put in an appearance but he further humiliated Naaman by insisting that he bathe in Israel's miserable river. Naaman had crossed the Jordan—a gray-green, greasy, sluggish body of water that looked like liquid mud. Indeed, the rivers of Damascus that ran from the snowfields of Lebanon were much more inviting. In outraged pride he stalked away from the word of God—unchanged.

But Naaman's servants intervened: "My father," they implored, "if the prophet had told you to do some great thing [literally, if the prophet's word had been a great word], would you not have done it?" (5:13).

So Naaman "went down and dipped himself in the Jordan . . . and his flesh was restored and became clean like that of a young boy" (5:14). The Hebrew text places "and he was clean" last.

A microscopic pathogen, a young girl, certain unknown attendants, and an unassuming prophet were the agents God used to bring about Naaman's humiliation and his cure. His response was worship: "Now I know," he said, "that there is no God in all the world except in Israel" (5:15).

The reason for the story in its original setting was to establish again the supremacy of Israel's God over all the gods. But I see another meaning: Here in Naaman's leprosy we see a picture of our sin and its cure.

We must "come down" to be healed. As long as we excuse our sin and cling to our rank and nobility, there is nothing God can do. But when we take our place as helpless and undone, then and only then are we in a place where God by His grace can cleanse us from all our iniquity.

We must fall at His feet. We must confess that we are "dust and ashes and full of sin." Then we are closest to Him, and He is able to set us free from all defilement and make us clean.

Like the flesh "of a young boy." Imagine that! Think of a mighty warrior with massive muscles rippling beneath the unblemished, unscarred flesh of a little child! This can be ours as well if we allow Jesus to pass His hands over our leprous lives. Though utterly ruined, we can return to the days of our youth—not merely forgiven, but cleansed as if none of our sins had ever occurred; not merely cleansed, but clad in newness of life and in the beauty of our Lord Jesus Christ.

—Seasoned with Salt

Wisdom Gained in Melancholy

*I tell you the truth, unless a kernel of wheat falls to the ground and
dies, it remains only a single seed. But if it dies, it produces many
seeds. The man who loves his life will lose it, while the man who
hates his life in this world will keep it for eternal life. Whoever
serves me must follow me; and where I am, my servant also will be.
My Father will honor the one who serves me.*
—John 12:24–26

I know melancholy. I've had my blue Mondays and my dark weeks. Oh, I enjoy long periods of heart-easing joy, but some mornings, for some reason, I find myself under a cloud.

A psychiatrist friend tells me that depression is usually the result of one of three factors: *loss, anger,* or *guilt.* I've often worked through his sources to find the root of my own gloom.

Loss is an inevitable part of life. We lose things all the time—keys, contact lenses, important papers and letters, lunker trout. Most of our losses are minor in the larger scheme of things.

Other losses, however, are catastrophic—death, cancer, rape, abuse; they take something from us that can never be replaced. One writer observed that while ordinary loss is like a broken arm, catastrophic loss is like an amputation: something is gone forever. Time does not heal all wounds.

Great sadness comes from catastrophic loss, and the root of that sorrow, it seems to me, is wanting something that we cannot have. At the risk of sounding indifferent and uncaring, the only way to deal with it is to let go of what you want but cannot have—to die to your right to enjoy good health, good friends, a trouble-free family environment, unconditional marital love, and golden retirement years. Dying is the only way to come alive.

Paul put it this way, "We always carry around in our body the death [or "dying"] of Jesus, so that the life of Jesus may also be revealed in our body. For we who are alive are always being given over to death for Jesus' sake, so that his life may be revealed in our mortal body" (2 Corinthians 4:10–11).

Paul's phrase "given over to death" refers to those losses and bereavements that cause us such deep sorrow. His answer is to "carry around in our body the [dying] of Jesus"; in other words, to adopt the attitude that Jesus brought to every loss: a willingness to give up what He wanted and submit to His Father's will—"Your way not Mine."

Jesus died every day of His life. The cross was simply the culmination of a lifetime of dying—to His dreams, His reputation, His career, His friends, His comfort, and eventually to His own life. Every day He gave up something He couldn't have. And so must we. "Die before you die," C. S. Lewis said, "there is no chance after."

Dying is hard. It was hard for Jesus, and it's hard for us, yet it is the means by which we know joy again—a greater joy than ever before. In fact, as I think about it, I wonder if we can ever know real joy until we have known profound loss, until all other sources of happiness have been eliminated by earthly sorrow and we have come to Jesus, that tireless Lover of our souls. He alone is the source of eternal consolation and joy. In Him we know an enjoyment not based on having what we want, but on having *Him*. To be without is an indispensable part of happiness—a happiness that "summer cannot wither and winter cannot chill." That's the enjoyment described in Habakkuk 3:17–18:

> Though the fig tree does not bud
> and there are no grapes on the vines,
> though the olive crop fails
> and the fields produce no food,
> though there are no sheep in the pen
> and no cattle in the stalls,
> yet I will rejoice in the Lord,
> I will be joyful in God my Savior.

Anger is another element that contributes to our gloom. Much has been written about the effect of rage, resentment, mistrust, hate, and suspicion on our peace of mind. All create unrest and depression.

Anger grows out of disappointment and hurt when our needs are not met. Our hurt becomes rage and resentment and then revenge—the desire to hurt back. There is no peace that way. The anger turns inward on us and crumples our souls. The inevitable result is depression.

Again, recovery means dying. It's a matter of letting go of self-will, of letting God do what He has purposed to do. It does not say, "Give me my rights!" but rather, "Lord, give me nothing but what You want"—like Isaac lying passively in the arms of his father, Abraham; like Mary consenting to her humiliation ("Let it be unto me according to Your will"); like David acquiescing in his pain ("Let Him do to me what seems best to Him").

Then there is a *guilt*, that still, small voice that makes us feel still smaller. What's the cure? To try to do better? No, this will only make us worse. The best thing for us is to do what God has been doing all along and forgive our ungodly selves. In a way it involves another kind of dying—putting to death our efforts to justify ourselves and purge our own consciences from sin.

Jesus defended His preoccupation with tax collectors and sinners by saying that He had not come to save the healthy but the sick. Of course we're sick and sinful; of course we've gone wrong. Yet we're forgiven. "Christ died for the *ungodly*" (Romans 5:6).

Our Lord's death, in which we participate by faith, was a death to sin. He paid sin's penalty on the cross and rose again to new life. "The death he died, he died to sin once for all; but the life he lives, he lives to God" (Romans 6:10).

Because we are identified with Christ in his death, burial, and resurrection, we too have new life. "The old has gone; the new has come!" (2 Corinthians 5:17). The old "sin question" has been settled. We will sin, but we are free from sin's consequences—its guilt, pollution, humiliation, and bondage.

There will always be acts to regret, apologies to make, mistakes that can never be corrected. There is, however, "no condemnation for those who are in Christ Jesus" (Romans 8:1), which means, among other things, that God does more than rid us of the *feelings* of guilt; he rids us of guilt itself!

We don't have to grieve any longer for anything we've said or done; we do not have to wallow in self-pity. We can confess our sins and move on.

At times it's hard for me to get that forgiveness out of my head and into my heart. The only way I know is to ask for it. Prayer is the means by which we translate truth into reality. There is no other way.

Loss, anger, and guilt all result in sorrow, but it seems to me there may be another element that contributes to it—one not understood by once-born men and women. It may be that our heartache is nothing more than home-sickness.

Broken homes, broken relationships, broken promises, broken bodies all remind us that this world is not our home. Heaven lies ahead, and there will always be some sorrow in us until we get there. Then (and only then) will God "wipe every tear from [our] eyes" (Revelation 21:4).

Finally, it has come to me in recent years that our dark moods, for all their aching discomfort, are in fact a grace disguised, for, whatever their cause, they can become the means by which God draws us into prayer and contemplation and thus into deep understanding. Blue is "staid wisdom's hue."

It's best to accept our gloom when it arrives, for steadfastly borne it can push us closer to God and give us more of the wisdom that comes from above.

—*In Quietness and Confidence*

" By His power God raised the Lord from the dead, and He will raise us also".
   1 Cor 6v14

When our bodies are redeemed + perfected, they'll display His beauty forever.

Putting the Body in Perspective

The body is not meant for sexual immorality,
but for the Lord, and the Lord for the body . . .
Therefore honor God with your body.
—1 Corinthians 6:13, 20

In Paul's day most philosophers believed that only the mind mattered or, more precisely, the things on which you put your mind mattered—the "Ideals." The body therefore was base, and either you got it into line or you gave up on it and went for all the gusto. Stoic or Epicurean, monk or a drunk, one was the same as the other. The body was bad.

Paul would disagree.

First, God is for the body—an idea that appeals to me as I get older and fewer parts work, and those that do work don't work as they used to. Saint Francis was right: "Brother Ass" is just the right name for one's body, often stubborn and always absurd. Yet Paul affirms that the Lord is for my body.

Second, the body is for the Lord. He not only loves it, but He has a purpose for it. Our bodies were made to contain the living God and make His invisible attributes known. Looks don't matter—tall, dark, and handsome; short, shot, and shapeless—our bodies are beautiful when they make His beauty known.

Furthermore, He has an eternal purpose for our bodies. This isn't all there is. "By his power God raised the Lord from the dead, and he will raise us also" (1 Corinthians 6:14). When our bodies are redeemed and perfected, they'll display His beauty forever. That's what bodies are everlastingly for.

Because our bodies have an eternal destiny, Paul maintains that we shouldn't misappropriate them now. They aren't made for self-indulgence and impurity. Sex is good, but illicit sex prostitutes our bodies. It's a sellout. He calls us to "flee from sexual immorality." As he puts it, "All other sins a man commits are outside his body, but he who sins sexually sins against his own body" (6:18). Sex outside of marriage is uniquely a sin against the body because it violates the purpose for which the body was made. Bodies aren't meant to be indulged on whim; they have a nobler purpose. They're made to contain God and display Him forever.

There was a saying in Corinth: "Food for the stomach and the stomach for food" (6:13), by which the Corinthians meant that nature demanded satisfaction. The stomach was made for food, and food was made for the body. When Mac-attacked, therefore, indulge oneself! True, Paul agreed, the body was made for food and food for the body, but we mustn't extrapolate from that principle to another—that the body was made for sex and sex for the body. No, the body is more than its parts and is made for more than sex and self-indulgence. It's a sanctuary intended for God and meant to house Him—a place where He can be seen and known.

This leads Paul to his bottom line: "Therefore honor God [manifest His glory] with your body" (6:20).

That's what bodies are for!

"But," you say, "why would He want *my* body? It's the source of almost everything that's wrong with me. It has a dirty mind, it's lazy and self-indulgent, it's been abused by drugs and booze and too much partying. It has a sexually transmitted disease. It's wasted and ruined!"

And yet God still wants your body. It doesn't need to be tanned, toned, and terrific for Him. He asks that you bring it to Him with its attendant problems so He can make something good of it.

Most of us don't know what to do with our bodies. We have a love-hate relationship with them—alternately trashing and treasuring them. They'll never truly please us until we give them to God. He made our bodies, and only He knows what they're for.

Give your body to Him, and He'll let you know how to use it. Given God's love for you and your body, it's the only reasonable thing to do.

—*The Strength of a Man*

We Must Choose Whom to Serve

*He said to me, "Son of man, have you seen what the elders of the
house of Israel are doing in the darkness, each at the shrine of
his own idol? They said, 'The Lord does not see us; the Lord has
forsaken the land.' "*
—Ezekiel 8:12

The prophet Ezekiel was swept away in a vision, transported to Jerusalem
to the temple, to the gate through which God's people came to worship.
And there, in the entry to the court, stood a vulgar, indecent idol described
literally as "an idol that makes God jealous."

The idol Ezekiel saw was a phallic symbol, a carved pillar representing the
worship of sex and everything associated with it. It stood opposite the *sheki-
nah,* the cloud that represented the presence of God among his people.

These forces still vie for our affection. On the one hand there is sexuality;
on the other hand, spirituality—the two most powerful forces in the world.
The thrill of lust always leads us away from God. Lust and love for God cannot co-exist. They are antagonistic; one displaces the other.

Every day we move between these two passions; every day we're forced to
choose whom we'll serve: God or Phallus? The choice we make is the choice
we take with us into our souls.

If we bow before God, He will begin to deal with all our other choices. If
we worship sex, it will enter into the secret places in our lives and corrupt
us. We will go from bad to worse. As the angel said to Ezekiel, in effect, "You
haven't seen anything yet!" (8:6).

Ezekiel was taken then to the entrance of the inner court where he discovered a hole in the wall, as though someone had been trying to gain entrance. He was told to start digging—and there he discovered a secret door.

God said, "Go in and see what they're doing in there." So Ezekiel peeked into the room.

First he saw dirty pictures scrawled all over the walls, like the graffiti you see on cubicle walls in public restrooms. Then he saw a group of men on their knees worshiping the drawings on the walls and saying to themselves, "The Lord does not see us" (8:12).

The Lord said to Ezekiel, "Have you seen what the elders of the house of Israel are doing in the darkness, each at the shrine of his own idol?" (8:12), using a word for *idol* that is often translated "imaginations" in the Old Testament.

Imagination is the image-making function of our minds, the remarkable ability we have to form mental images with thoughts even though actual objects are out of sight. It's a promising faculty, but one we can prostitute, making the pictures pornographic, playing at sex in our heads, bedding down in that secret boudoir in our brains.

The first images tend to be ill defined, but we have the capacity to sharpen the focus and portray the pictures in vivid color and live action on the walls of our minds. Then they become memories, indelibly inscribed drawings to which we return again and again for worship. With each visit the pictures gain greater definition. All this goes on in those secret places from which we have excluded God.

Sexual fantasies are sins we readily excuse. Who knows, who cares, and who gets hurt? A victimless crime—or so we think. But sin always bears bitter fruit in us and in others. We cannot long contain its effects; it always breaks out in greater defilement. As the angel said again to Ezekiel, "You will see them doing things that are even more detestable!" (8:13). The result, as Ezekiel went on to see, is a slow sort of dying.

There is deliverance from this. We must choose whether we'll serve God or Phallus. It's a choice we make every day.

And then we must invite God into every part of our lives, even into those darkened rooms in our minds where we have our own four walls—rooms that we have staked out for ourselves and from which we have excluded Him. He will enter in, the entrance of His words will give light, the images on the walls will begin to fade, and He will write His own thoughts in their place. Our love for Him will be restored, and we will once again be the men God has created us to be.

—*In Quietness and Confidence*

image of the penis-That They were bowing down To.

Service Rendered to God

Whatever you do, work at it with all your heart, as working for the Lord, not for men.
—Colossians 3:23

If you're like most men, you probably need a good reason to get up on Monday morning and go to work. Your tasks may be menial and mindless, offering little challenge or stimulation. The sameness of it all has taken away any good reason for doing what you do. What you need is a philosophy of work that will get you going in the morning.

We labor in a fallen world. The ground works hard because it's cursed (Genesis 3:17–19). Creation grinds on in discord, our enemy more often than our ally, and no amount of work can change that much. Trying to beat the effects of the Fall simply turns us into workaholics. We think someday our labor will pay off, but it never does. Thorns and thistles keep cropping up in our field.

Sin makes everyone and everything more difficult; other men become our competitors, bent on grabbing our chips. They want to beat us out of our hard-earned money.

And apart from what sin has done to others, it's done something to us. We have a lazy streak. R & R is more important than work. If we work at all, it's to have more leisure, more time in our boat or our condo. Work is merely to buy more time away from work.

Because we've mostly left God out of our lives, work has become our substitute for security and significance. Our feelings of self-worth are tied to our work. That's why upward mobility is so important; more pay and greater prestige make us feel better about ourselves. And that's why failure is so devastating to our egos.

But regeneration changes how we perceive ourselves in relation to our work. We begin to learn that security and significance come from God, not what we do. We're special apart from the work we do. He loves us even if we're out of work. And when we begin to see ourselves as He sees us, we don't need work to feel worthy. Then work becomes valuable, not as a means to an end but as an end in itself.

Work is valuable in itself because God works. He's a hard worker and One who does His work well. He's known for His work. When we too do our work well, when our craftsmanship is sound and our products are well constructed and worthwhile, we're more like God.

Trivial and shoddy work, done solely for profit, diminishes us. Money costs too much when we have to make it that way. We should ask of a job, "Is it any good?" rather than, "What does it pay?" And we should ask about a finished product, "Is it worth buying?" rather than, "How can I get people to buy it?" As Dorothy Sayers said, "Serve the work! If your heart is not wholly in the work, the work will not be good—and work that is not good serves neither God nor the community; it only serves Mammon."

Work is valuable in itself because work can be service rendered to God. In all our work we work for Him, and no service rendered to Him is trivial. He sees and it matters to Him. This gives worth to everything we do, even those things no one else notices or appreciates. Michelangelo, painting in some dark corner on the Sistine ceiling, was asked by his helper why he was investing so much time and effort in a part of the painting that no one would ever see. "God will see!" he said.

The job we left last Friday remains the same, but it can have new meaning on Monday morning. Our work is significant no matter what we do. We work because God does; we're more like Him when we do. And we're working for our Lord, an employer who sees and approves. In this frame of mind, we can whistle while we work.

—The Strength of a Man

The Beauty of Holiness

At that time David was in the stronghold [of Adullam], and the Philistine garrison was at Bethlehem. David longed for water and said, "Oh, that someone would get me a drink of water from the well near the gate of Bethlehem!" So the three mighty men broke through the Philistine lines, drew water from the well near the gate of Bethlehem and carried it back to David. But he refused to drink it; instead, he poured it out before the Lord. "Far be it from me, O Lord, to do this!" he said. "Is it not the blood of men who went at the risk of their lives?" And David would not drink it.
—2 Samuel 23:14–17

This remarkable story about David tells me more about "the man after God's own heart" than any other description.

This event is placed in the text as one example of the love and loyalty of David's tough little army and the quality of David's life that drew good men around him.

The event occurred during the last stages of David's conflict with the Philistines, his mortal enemy. Cut off from the northern tribes from which he drew much of his support, David's situation seemed hopeless.

In a moment of homesickness and deep yearning for a former, less complicated time, David uttered a quiet wish for a drink from a well near Bethlehem he recalled from his youth. It was just a wish, nothing more, but three of his men heard him and took him at his word.

Without a word these men crept out of the stronghold at Adullam, fought their way through the Philistine lines to the well on the northeast side of the city of Bethlehem, drew water, fought their way back to David, and presented him with their gift.

David looked at the blood and bruises on their bodies and poured out the water as an offering to the Lord. It had cost too much; it was too precious to drink.

After reading about David and his mighty men with a couple of my friends one day, one of the men in the group leaned back in his chair and muttered to himself, "What a beautiful guy."

"Beautiful" sounded odd to me at the time, especially when applied to a rugged old warrior like David, but it's exactly the right word. The Bible itself speaks of "the beauty of holiness" (Psalm 29:2; 96:9 KJV) as though true goodness is something beautiful to see. It is. Peter put it this way: "Live such good lives among the pagans that, though they accuse you of doing wrong, they may see your good deeds and glorify God on the day he visits us" (1 Peter 2:12). The word twice translated "good" in this text means "beautiful." In that sense David was indeed a "beautiful guy."

The best way to see the true beauty of manhood is to see it in Jesus. Those who knew him best said that He was a good man, "full of grace and truth." Everything He did was truthful, and yet He was unfailingly gracious.

There is "truth" that isn't gracious at all. It may be the antithesis of falsehood, but it's also the antithesis of beauty. It was grace linked with truth that made Jesus the man He was.

I think of that occasion on which His disciples were arguing about who was the greatest. Who could have blamed our Lord if He had blasted them? But He did not. He rather girded Himself with a towel and washed their feet. He who was the greatest of all became the servant of all. Don't you think His disciples thought, *What a beautiful man*?

And then there was that leper Jesus encountered when He was teaching in one of the little villages of Galilee. Luke 5:12 (KJV) says the man was "full of leprosy"—a medical expression for an advanced case of the disease. He was all lesions, running sores, and grotesque stumps, discolored and disfigured, shocking in his ugliness, a gross caricature of what a man was intended to be.

Jesus, moved with compassion, reached out and hugged him. He didn't have to touch him. He could have cured the man with a word from afar. Yet there was every need in the world to hug this ugly, awful man because no one else had done so. Don't you think that man went away thinking, *What a beautiful man*?

I think of the dirty little street urchins of that day who used to tag along behind Jesus and climb into His lap, and I remember the adage that a truly good man is one "around whose gate and garden children are unafraid to play." His disciples wanted to shoo them away. Jesus gathered them into His arms and blessed them. Don't you think they remembered Him as a beautiful man?

These vignettes reflect a manly beauty that's hard to put into words. It's more than being decent, ethical, and right. It has a rugged, "more than" quality about it that Jesus summed up with the question, "What are you doing more than others?" (Matthew 5:47). It's a matter of doing things beautifully.

True goodness is not doing extraordinary things. It is doing ordinary things in an extraordinary way. Pascal said, "The strength of a man's virtue must not be measured by his efforts but by his ordinary life." It is not so much a matter of overt religious behavior as it is a gracious, winsome spirit with which we do everything.

Jesus was inclined to be very stern with those who wore their religion on their sleeves: "Be careful not to do your 'acts of righteousness' before men, to be seen by them," He warned. "If you do, you will have no reward from your Father in heaven" (Matthew 6:1). We'll never hear God's "Atta boy!" that way.

Authentic goodness is something more subtle. Howard Butt described it this way: "It is not a way of doing special things. It is a special way of doing everything." It's how we play the game: how we conduct ourselves when we play a round of golf; how we behave ourselves at a business conference; how we talk to our wives and our children; how we respond to slights and injustices. It is doing everything we do with a certain elegance and style.

I'm reminded of a friend of mine, Brian Morgan, who went to Stanford University in the 1970s with hopes of becoming an Olympic gymnast. Someone had planted Paul's word in his mind, "Glorify God in your body" (1 Corinthians 6:20 KJV). His plan was to hone his body to perfection and then, having achieved a certain measure of athletic prominence, give God all the credit for his success. But Brian was an athlete who matured early and got no better. In fact, he got worse. His senior year was a disaster.

The coup de grâce came at an NCAA meet when he fell off the high bar and landed on his head. It was hard on his head but good for his soul, he said. That's when it came to him that what Paul actually said was, glorify God in your body, not with it. It was far more important for him to be gracious in dishonor than to win big and look good. It's that subtle shift in thought that represents the beauty of holiness.

We cannot, by moral effort, change ourselves one iota. Everything that needs to be done in our souls can only be done by God. "All virtue is a miracle," said Augustine.

Change creeps to us. It is the fruit of our association with Jesus. As we draw close to Him day by day—walking with Him, talking to Him, listening to His words, relying on Him, asking for His help—His character begins to rub off on us. Quietly and unobtrusively His influence softens our wills, making us thirsty for His righteousness. In His quiet love He takes all that's unworthy in us and gradually turns it into something beautiful.

We cannot adorn ourselves. "You adorn yourself in vain," says Jeremiah 4:30. Rather, with David, we can only "gaze upon the beauty of the Lord" (Psalm 27:4) and ask Him to transform us into His image, from one degree of likeness to the next.

"O Lord, help me!" This is our prayer as well.

—A Man to Match the Mountain

Follow Through

Not that I have already obtained all this,
or have already been made perfect, but I press on to take hold of
that for which Christ Jesus took hold of me. Brothers, I do not
consider myself yet to have taken hold of it. But one thing I do:
Forgetting what is behind and straining toward what is ahead, I
press on toward the goal to win the prize for which God has called
me heavenward in Christ Jesus.
All of us who are mature should take such a view of things. And if
on some point you think differently, that too God
will make clear to you. Only let us live up to what
we have already attained.
—Philippians 3:12–16

I often think to myself: If only I could get it together—make one brilliant assault on the powers of evil and overthrow them forever. If only I could take one stand in the face of temptation and resist it so that sin's attractions would fade away. If only there were some cabalistic ceremony, some mystic utterance that would exorcise for all time the demons of lust, fear, pride, and greed. If only . . . if only . . . if only . . .

Instead of a quick fix and final perfection, however, I find myself locked in a tedious struggle against bedeviling sins, an arduous ordeal in which resistance seems to make only the slightest impression. Everything I reform soon returns to its old configuration.

I defeat one sin only to find another rising up to assault me. I resist one temptation only to develop more subtle tendencies. I subdue one humiliating behavior only to have it return suddenly and without warning in another mortifying display. Frankly, it does me a lot of good to hear Paul say, of all the sinners in the world, "I am the worst" (1 Timothy 1:15). I always thought I was.

I used to think that age would rid me of sin, that someday I would simply outgrow it, but that's a fool's dream. The passing years have not done away with sin but rather have deepened my perception of it. What I once thought of as peccadilloes I now see as perversions. So much of me is yet unconverted.

I see shades of evil in me now that a former knowledge of God failed to reveal: subtle omissions; ungodly attitudes and orientations; hidden areas of self-interest and self-protection; destructive ways of relating to others; defensive ways of covering up; entrenched areas of self-confidence; deep-seated hungers for human approval; tendencies to gain my identity and worth from things other than God. There comes a time, John Bunyan reminds us, when we enter a region along the frontier where "the contrast between the bride and the Bridegroom is heightened and oft-times renewed."

One thing I've learned: It does no good to "should" myself—urge myself to various and sundry abstinences or exhort myself to hustle more in the hope that I can make holiness happen. As Luther said, "We are conquered if we try conscientiously not to sin." Laying the law on ourselves doesn't work—at least not for very long. Such efforts may have "an appearance of wisdom . . . but they lack any value in restraining sensual indulgence" over the long haul (Colossians 2:23).

The Law *is* good—don't misunderstand me. It can show us where we've gone wrong, but it has no mechanism for overriding our natural tendency to *do* wrong. It was never meant to cure us; it can only make our disobedience seem worse and make us feel even more guilty. Bunyan, in *The Pilgrim's Progress*, personifies the Law as Moses, who greets his followers and beats them with a stick. "I know not how to show mercy," he shouts.

No, it's not exhortations to try harder or do better that I need. What's needed is the power to behave as I already know I should. Walter Brueggerman speaks for all of us when he writes, "I have found myself discovering that mostly I do not need more advice, but strength. I do not need new information, but the courage, freedom, and authorization to act on what I already have been given in the gospel."

So, I ask myself, "What is this 'courage, freedom, and authorization to act on what I have been given in the gospel'? What is the dynamic for change? What can I do to be more like my Lord?"

In the words of a song I vaguely recall—

> I've got the want to,
> I need the *follow through.*

One odd thing about the process is that things usually get worse before they get better. At first, instead of becoming more like Jesus, we're likely to be shown more of our disconformity. Not to worry, however. God shows us our ungodliness only as He gives us the courage to bear the sight of it.

Furthermore, His purpose in exposing us is always good: it's useful for us to see our true character; that way we are driven to hope in God rather than ourselves.

God knows us profoundly, and He knows the exact source of our troubles. His hand strikes in unexpected places and leaves nothing uncovered. "As long as the least bit of self-love remains in the secret parts of our heart," Fenelon said, "God will hunt it down, and by some merciful blow, force our selfishness and jealousy out of hiding."

He does so not to curse us, but to cure us—to drive us to Him that we might find our all in His care. There's more at stake, you see, than mere holiness. God wants most of all to have our love.

I ask you—those of you who are fathers—would you rather have a child who was struggling and clinging to you in love or one who had it all together and never gave you the time of day? I think the former description represents more of what our Father's heart longs for. Oh, He will make us good children soon enough, but first of all He wants our affection.

Here's the main thing: If we are to be changed at all, it must be God who does the changing. Change is God's gift to His children. He wants it for us, and it is His nature to give it. George MacDonald asks, "Are you able to worship a God who will give you all the little things He does not care about, but will not give you help to do the things He wants you to do, but which you do not know how to do?" Or as Jesus put it, "If you, then, though you are evil, know how to give good gifts to your children, how much more will your Father in heaven give good gifts to those who *ask* him" (Matthew 7:11).

We must ask God to change us—give Him all that's wrong with us and wait for His working.

Oh, there are other things we can do—meditate on His Word and seek His will with a determination to do it; think deeply about ourselves and the underlying causes of our behavior; avoid people and situations that are ruinous to our souls; worship with God's people and look to them for intercession, encouragement, and support. These things work on us to draw us ever more deeply into His heart and into His hands. In the end only He can change us and make us what we were meant to be. "The one who has called you is faithful and *he* will do it!" (1 Thessalonians 5:24).

It comes to this: We can try to achieve righteousness on our own, or we can receive it. The one makes us uptight because we're never good enough to satisfy ourselves; the other makes us grateful for any progress we've made.

Are you dissatisfied with yourself? Do you hate your sin and long to do better? Then you are of the same mind with God, and you can ask Him to bring growth to you, "first the stalk, then the ear, then the full grain in the ear." He is very strong toward those whose hearts are like His (2 Chronicles 16:9). We may despair of ourselves (that, it seems, is inevitable), but we should never despair of God. He is out to mature us.

But we must know this: Maturity, when it comes, will come in its own time and way. We want to look over God's shoulder and see how we're doing, chart our progress, put limits on the process, and in other ways direct it. But that is not our business. Our job is to follow the Lord in humility and simplicity and keep ourselves open to what He is doing in and around us. We must give in to Him with a humble heart and let Him work everything out for us.

When God directs the work, He goes straight for the center of what He hates most in us. It may not be the thing we hate—some disgusting habit that annoys others and humiliates us—but rather something we hold most dear.

He may overlook some flaw we despise and concentrate His work instead on other matters we care less about. He may permit some unsavory habit to linger, "loathed and long," to lead us into humility. He may leave trace elements of the old life—"Canaanites" in the land—so He can teach us how to wage holy war (Judges 3:2).

God alone knows what matters need to be addressed and in what order. Let God do what seems right to Him. Press on in the confidence that His processes are adequate to deal with your sin, asking for His help and offering yourself up to His will, content (though never satisfied) until we "take hold of that for which Christ Jesus took hold of [us]" (Philippians 3:12).

Ponder this gracious assurance: "That our God may count you worthy of his calling, and that by his power he may fulfill every good purpose of yours and every act prompted by your faith" (2 Thessalonians 1:11). He has instilled in you the desire to do better. He who prompted the desire is able to fulfill it.

In the meantime, while you wait for His perfect work, don't worry about your failures. Offer up to God all that worries and annoys you and wait for Him in peace.

Phyllis McGinley wrote, "The wonderful thing about saints is that they were human. They lost their tempers, scolded God, were egotistical or testy or impatient in their turns, made mistakes and regretted them. Still they went on doggedly blundering toward heaven."

So blunder on. Don't dwell on present failings or on the dead past. Every day has its mishaps and memories of something we should have done or not done. "Never look back" must be our motto. Press on! Though in process and incomplete, we are freely loved, fully forgiven, and on our way to glory. Sin may frustrate us for a day, but God's favor goes on forever, and on ahead lays perfection. Someday soon we shall see God face to face, and we shall be like Him—"holy as the Holy One."

"Rivers know this," Winnie the Pooh assures us. "There is no hurry. We shall get there some day."

—*In Quietness and Confidence*

Persistence That Pays

Many a man claims to have unfailing love,
but a faithful man who can find?
—Proverbs 20:6

Some of my friends are steelhead fishermen, which means, of course, that I'm occasionally obliged to join them in their pursuit of that wily game-fish. I always do it against my better judgment.

The question comes to me, standing waist-deep in icy water, dodging ice floes and trying to cast a fly line into the teeth of gale-force winds: Why would any creature with an IQ higher than a slab of concrete want to do this to himself, particularly when he hardly ever catches a fish? They tell me steel-headers average one fish every twenty hours or so. I'm the guy who brings the average down for the whole crowd. However, as they say, once you catch a steelhead, life is never the same!

I'll say this for steelheaders: They are persistent! Good steelhead fisher-men never give up. They have a Job-like patience that puts the rest of the world to shame. So, as in most good pursuits, patience and persistence are the name of the game.

Once upon a time we believed that nothing worthwhile came easily. Today it's assumed that almost anything ought to be done quickly and with very little effort. In such a world it isn't hard to get started, but it sure is hard to endure for very long. When the novelty wears off, our interest wears thin. There's a market for all kinds of experience, but little enthusiasm for the patient acquisition of anything arduous, little inclination to sign up for any-thing that's long-term and hard.

But being authentically Christian is often just a matter of making hard choices and sticking with them because we know that what God asks is for our good. "The essential thing," as Friedrich Nietzsche said, "is that there should be a long obedience in the same direction; there thereby results, and has always resulted in the long run, something which has made life worth living."

Real Christianity means giving ourselves to everyday, low-profile obedience—an activity for which we get the least encouragement from our hustling peers. Other people initially have more flash; they are euphoric whirlwinds of activity as long as things go well. But then they encounter pain and resistance, and they fold. They are sensual people—governed by feelings rather than by the Word.

What's required of us, on the other hand, is dogged determined endurance, keeping at the task of following Jesus through life's ebbs and flows, ups and downs, whether we feel like it or not, knowing that it's God "who works in [us] to will and to act according to his good purpose" (Philippians 2:13). We won't get everything right—we're only human—but God sees the heart and knows its intent, and He encourages every effort to comply. He's dogged in His endurance too, and wonderfully persistent. He never gives up on us.

Paul said, "It is required that those who have been given a trust must prove faithful" (1 Corinthians 4:2). Not always successful. Just faithful. It is necessary then that we keep showing up, willing to do what our Lord is asking us to do, however difficult it may be. Slowly, staunchly, steadfastly—that's how every hard task is finally done.

Woody Allen was right: "Eighty percent of life is just showing up."

—*A Burden Shared*

PART 3

Pursuing Love and Peace

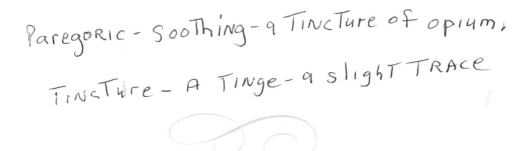

Paregoric - Soothing - a Tincture of opium,

Tincture - A Tinge - a slight Trace

Being That Kind of Person

My fellow prisoner Aristarchus sends you his greetings,
as does Mark, the cousin of Barnabas . . . Jesus, who is called
Justus, also sends greetings. These are the only Jews among
my fellow workers for the kingdom of God, and they
have proved a comfort to me.
—Colossians 4:10–11

Mitigate - help Take Away

Paul wrote of certain friends who, he said, "have proved a comfort to me." The word *comfort* is an unusual word, a medical term Paul may have picked up from his good friend Dr. Luke. This is the only place it occurs in the New Testament.

In Paul's day the verb *comfort* meant "to alleviate pain." We get the archaic term *paregoric* from it, a word my mother used to apply to some mysterious and wondrous potion in our medicine chest.

Paul couldn't have used a better word. What could be more encouraging than to know that there are people like that: men and women who alleviate and mitigate our pain?

Pain is one of the necessities of life. No one evades it. Physical discomfort is hard to bear, but it seems to me that the greatest pain comes from the heart: the pain of weakness and shame; the pain of misunderstanding, criticism, and accusation; the pain of deferred hope, disillusionment, and abandoned dreams; the pain of lonely isolation.

Unfortunately there are those sincere but much too certain people who only add to our pain. Like Job's comforters, they talk too much and have a reason for everything that comes our way. They leave us more uncomfortable than before.

On the other hand, there are those good and honest souls who, like Paul's friends, alleviate our pain. Often they're simple, humble people, not in the least important or distinguished, yet somehow, in the wear and tear of life, they always find a way to reduce our discomfort. It's not that they say very much; it's just that they're there and care and listen well and pray. Most times that's all a body needs.

At other times it's the way they bear their own pain. Their sorrow, endured in simple faith, helps us to bear ours. Their affliction, endured courageously, helps us to be a little braver.

Often they're not even aware of the comfort they bring to us. They're unconscious of any effect because they aren't trying to have an effect. They're just being what they are—a comfort.

You say, "I'd like to be that kind of person." Not to worry. If you're spending time in devotion to God and growing toward likeness to Him, you will be a comfort to others whether you know it or not. It's not something you try to do. It's something that happens when you're hiding yourself in Him.

It may be that someday someone will write you a letter as Paul did and say, "You were a comfort to me." Maybe not. Some folks never think to tell you what you've done for them or thank you for your consolation. But God knows, and that's all that matters.

—In Quietness and Confidence

Learning to Listen

Oh, that I had someone to hear me!
—Job 31:35

René Descarte, the sixteenth-century philosopher, said, "I think, therefore I am." Sarah, our granddaughter, says, "You are, therefore I talk."

Some years ago I was sitting in our family room trying to read a *Time* magazine while Sarah was trying to carry on a conversation with me. To my shame I was paying little attention, responding to her comments with an occasional grunt.

Finally, in exasperation, she crawled into my lap and got in my face: "Papa," she shouted, "are you listening to me?"

"Sarah," I confessed, putting down my magazine, "I haven't been listening well. Forgive me. I'll listen to you now."

That's a commitment I want to keep on other occasions as well. I want to learn how to listen.

I want to listen well so that when I finish conversations others will walk away knowing there's at least one person in this careless world who has some inkling of what they're doing, thinking, and feeling. I want to hear the hushed undertones of their hearts. I want them to know that I care.

Listening, however, doesn't come easy for me. I'm paid to talk—a "word-monger," to borrow Augustine's apt description of a teacher. So it has come as something of a revelation to me that I can do more with my ears than I can with my mouth.

In her book *Listening to Others*, Joyce Huggett relates personal experiences of listening to suffering people. She said they often talk about all she's done for them. "On many occasions," she wrote, "I have not 'done' anything. I have 'just listened.' I quickly came to the conclusion that 'just listening' was indeed an effective way of helping others."

This was the help Job's wordy, would-be friends failed to give him. They were "miserable comforters," he complained. "Oh, that I had someone to hear me!" (Job 16:2; 31:35).

Job's friends weren't listening. They didn't hear what he had to say. In fact, he wasn't even sure God was listening.

Job is not alone in his longing. All human beings want to be heard, and listening is one of the best ways in the world to love them. Listening says, "You matter to me; I want to be a friend."

Kenneth Grahame's Badger in *The Wind in the Willows* knew exactly how to do this: "He sat in his arm-chair at the head of the table, and nodded gravely at intervals as the animals told their story; and he did not seem surprised or shocked at anything, and he never said, 'I told you so,' or, 'Just what I always said,' or remarked that they ought to have done so-and-so, or ought not to have done something else. The Mole began to feel very friendly towards him."

Listening is a lost art these days. We don't listen well, and we aren't used to being listened to. Most of our words simply fall to the ground.

I have a friend who, when he goes to noisy parties and people ask how he's doing, on occasion has replied quietly, "My business went belly-up this week, the bank foreclosed on my house, my wife left me, and I have terminal cancer." "Wonderful!" one man murmured, as he pumped my friend's hand and moved on. I keep wondering if I've done the same thing to others in other ways.

Here are some things I'm learning about listening:

- When I'm thinking about an answer while others are talking—I'm not listening.
- When I give unsolicited advice—I'm not listening.
- When I suggest they shouldn't feel the way they do—I'm not listening.
- When I apply a quick fix to their problem—I'm not listening.
- When I fail to acknowledge their feelings—I'm not listening.
- When I fidget, glance at my watch, and appear to be rushed—I'm not listening.
- When I fail to maintain eye contact—I'm not listening.
- When I don't ask follow-up questions—I'm not listening.
- When I top their story with a bigger, better story of my own—I'm not listening.

- When they share a difficult experience and I counter with one of my own—I'm not listening.

Listening is hard work and most of us are unwilling to put in the time, and time is required. Listening means setting aside our own timetable and tendency to hurry on to our next destination. It means settling into a re-laxed, unhurried, leisurely pace. "Only in the ambience of leisure," Eugene Peterson wrote, "do persons know they are listened to with absolute serious-ness, treated with dignity and importance."

In leisure we regard one another's interests as more important than ours (Philippians 2:3). In leisure we say, "You are more significant than anything I have to do right now. You are the only one who counts, the one for whom I am willing to forget my other obligations, appointments, and meetings. I have time for you." In leisure we listen long enough to hear the other person's true heart, so that if we do speak, we speak with gentle wisdom.

A leisurely pace, a listening ear, a loving heart—these are the qualities of a good conversationalist. Would that you and I, by God's grace, will acquire them.

A final caveat: Even if you listen well, most folks won't make that effort in return. We've all had the experience of leaving a long conversation aware that we know a great deal about the other person but they know almost nothing about us. "Be patient," Winnie the Pooh says. "If people don't listen, it may be that they have a small piece of fluff in their ear."

—Out of the Ordinary

Pro-Life in the Purest Sense

Your eyes saw my unformed body.
All the days ordained for me
were written in your book
before one of them came to be.
　　　　　　　　—Psalm 139:16

Second Kings 4:8–17 begins a story of Elisha and a wealthy Shunammite woman. One day Elisha asked her, "What can I do for you?"

"I have a home among my own people" she replied, an idiom that suggests quiet contentment.

But Gehazi, Elisha's servant, detected a deep sorrow she was unwilling to share. "She has no son," he observed, "and her husband is old" (4:13–14).

Childlessness was a cause for deep regret and social reproach in the ancient world. Jacob's wife Rachel, speaking for many childless couples even now, cried out: "Give me children, or I'll die!" (Genesis 30:1).

Elisha, being a prophet and understanding God's intentions, promised the Shunammite woman that she would hold a child in her arms, "about this season, according to the time of life," as the King James Version says (4:16). The text is difficult and has mystified many, but it suggests that the miracle consisted of a normal sequence of conception according to the woman's cycle and nine-month gestation; the process appeared normal in every way. This reminds me that every delivery is a miracle, even those for which we think that everything depends upon us. Though a natural process appears to be at work, it is God who forms the fetus in the womb (see Isaiah 49:5; Jeremiah 1:5).

Since I first read G. K. Chesterton's *Orthodoxy,* I have been intrigued by his idea that God is still creating the world and everything in it. He proposed that just as a child delights in seeing a thing done again and again, God delights in the repetition and "monotony" of creation every day. "It is possible that God says every morning, 'Do it again' to the sun; and every evening, 'Do it again' to the moon. It may not be automatic necessity that makes all daisies alike; it may be that God makes every daisy separately, but has never got tired of making them . . . The repetition in Nature may not be a mere recurrence; it may be a theatrical ENCORE!"

It is possible that every new emergence—every blade of grass, every butterfly, every billowing cloud—is a new and special creation invented out of God's wisdom, excitement, and artistry. He paints each pansy as it emerges in the spring. He colors every leaf in the fall. He ponders every act of creation, shouts "encore!" and the whole business begins all over again, the business of creation that began "in the beginning" and is still going on to this day.

Thus, by analogy, every human conception is a creation. God says, "Let us make humankind in our image, according to our likeness"—and human life springs into being! We think of the process as purely natural; we conceive a child, and it grows to term on its own. In truth it is preternatural—*a miraculous creation.* (It occurs to me at the same time that any given conception might be God's final creation, in which case the human race would very soon be extinct, for our existence, despite our heroic efforts to perpetuate ourselves, is solely dependent on God's creative handiwork.)

Chesterton suggested the idea of ongoing creation to me, but David, Israel's poet, convinced me, for he described God first "musing" and then "weaving" David together in the darkness of his mother's womb. He did so, David insisted, "before one of them [the various elements that became 'David'] came to be [were in existence]" (Psalm 139:13–16). The Hebrew text for verse 16 reads: "Your eyes saw my unformed substance and in Your book they [David's 'component parts'] were written day by day before there was one of them." The metaphor is that of a "journal" in which God wrote His ideas of what David would become and then brought each idea into being through His handiwork in the womb.

In other words, God created David out of nothing—no, out of Himself. He imagined the person who was to be and then brought that person into being according to a preimagined plan.

Put another way, we begin as a gleam in our heavenly Father's eye and are shaped by Love into a unique, immediate creation—immediate in the ordinary sense of "unmediated," in that we come directly from the inventive heart and hand of God.

That means that I am special and so are you—and so is everyone else in the world. This being true, I must be pro-life in the purest sense of the word in that I sanctify *all* human life[4]—Stanford University sophisticates and untutored semi-illiterates, Seattle socialites and skid-row derelicts, winsome children and doddering curmudgeons, fundamentalist preachers and left-wing political pundits, Muslims and Christians, homosexuals and heterosexuals, antiabortion enthusiasts and pro-choice activists. Every person—of any class, age, sex, and race—is a unique production of our Creator's genius.

Which is why Jesus said we should never call anyone a "fool."[5]

—Seasoned with Salt

---

4. The Bible supports the sanctity of human life and not life in general, for human beings alone are created in the image and likeness of God, that is, more like God than any other creatures.
5. Matthew 5:22. His word here means "worthless."

If I Had a Hammer

Most blessed of women be Jael,
the wife of Heber the Kenite,
most blessed of tent-dwelling women.
—Judges 5:24

Dorothy Sayers claimed that Sigmund Freud's question, "What does a woman want?" is frivolous. "What is unreasonable and irritating is to assume that all one's tastes and preferences have to be conditioned by the class to which one belongs."

For her, the appropriate question is not, "What do women want?" but rather, "What does *this* woman want?" "Are all women created to do the same thing?" she asked. "The obvious answer is no, of course not. Never in the course of history and least of all now. Men and women are created to do a special thing in the world. Their task is to find that thing."

Which brings me to the story of Jael and the "special thing" she was created to do.

In the days of the judges, Sisera was the commander of the Canaanite army. His army was heavily armed with nine hundred iron chariots. But God gave the Israelites the victory. "All the troops of Sisera fell by the sword; not a man was left"—except Sisera, who fled on foot north toward Hazor, his command post (Judges 4:16). He had almost reached safety when he came upon a Kenite camp.

Sisera had every reason to expect sanctuary with the Kenites. They were a friendly tribe that honored the ancient rules and conventions of hospitality in that part of the world. So Sisera fled to the tent of Heber, the head of the tribe. There Jael, Heber's wife, welcomed him.

The writer describes the scene in detail: Jael invites Sisera in, and when he tells her he is thirsty, she gives him "thickened milk," a yogurt drink that was mildly soporific. She then hides him under a blanket where the thoroughly frightened and exhausted man drops off to sleep—a sleep from which he never awakens.

While he slumbers Jael takes a tent peg and the mallet with which the pegs were driven into the ground and hammers the stake through Sisera's head!

Soon Barak, the Israeli commander who is pursuing Sisera, comes by the camp. Jael goes out to meet him and leads him to her tent, lifts the flap, and shows him the gory sight.

As the judge and prophetess Deborah had predicted, the honor of the victory was not Barak's, for the Lord had delivered Sisera into a woman's hands (Judges 4:9).

On that day Deborah sang a song commemorating Jael's deed:

> Her hand reached for the tent peg,
>   her right hand for the workman's hammer.
> She struck Sisera, she crushed his head,
>   she shattered and pierced his temple (5:26).

In those words you can hear the lethal hammer blows! Jael, the Terminator!

There's something terrible and grand about this woman: terrible because we wince at her bloody act; grand because we witness her zeal for God. Jael's savage sledge was a hammer of justice, and from that day on "the hand of the Israelites grew stronger and stronger against Jabin, the Canaanite king, until they destroyed him" (4:24). Her heroic act was the beginning of the end of Canaanite control, and thus Israel, the repository of the "seed" of our salvation, was spared.

"Most blessed of women be Jael," Deborah sang, a phrase reminiscent of Elizabeth's blessing of Mary, the mother of Jesus. And what did Jael do to merit such praise? She did the thing she was created to do.

Admittedly not many women (or men, for that matter) are called to carry out such violent acts. Most of our obedience comes in the ordinary affairs of everyday life. But we never know what heroism lies in quiet obedience to God, and there's no biblical reason why a woman, in her obedience, may not play an extraordinary role in the unfolding drama of world redemption.

In his book *I Francis*, Carlo Carretto, the twentieth-century Italian theologian and mystic, wrote: "Today, a woman must hear the words of Jesus as a man hears them; and if Jesus says, 'Go and make disciples of all nations,' it must no longer be that a man hears this in one way and a woman in another . . .

"Do not copy men. Be authentic. Seek, in your femaleness, the root that distinguishes you from them. It is unmistakable, for it has been willed and created by God himself. Repeat to yourselves every day: A man is not a woman."

Women are fully equal to men in their capacity to know God, to learn from Him, and to do what He calls them to do. So (and here I speak to women), seek in your created role as a woman the "root that distinguishes you" and follow Jesus. You cannot imagine where He will take you and what He will do with you there, but I can tell you this: He is "able to do immeasurably more than all [you] ask or imagine, according to his power that is at work within [you]" (Ephesians 3:20).

I say then to us men, when we belittle women and minimize their abilities, when we attempt to curb their God-given gifts and creativity and restrict their service, when we think that women, merely because they are women, will reason irrationally, act irresponsibly, or fold under pressure, we've missed what is said again and again in God's Word. There is "neither . . . male nor female" (Galatians 3:28). When it comes to doing God's will, the differences between men and women—whatever they are—make no difference at all.

—*Out of the Ordinary*

There is "neither . . . male nor female"
Gal 3v28

Guarding Ourselves Against Adultery

Why be captivated, my son, by an adulteress?
Why embrace the bosom of another man's wife?
—Proverbs 5:20

I keep seeing my friends fall. I wonder why they do it. What causes men and women to trash their marriages for a transient affair? Why would we give our strength to others and fill our old age with regret (Proverbs 5:9)?

Perhaps it's naiveté. We think we're invincible, like Samson. Samson was a fool, and so are we if we believe that we will never fall. Everyone is temptable; everyone has a price. The key is to know how vulnerable we are and always be on the alert. We're overthrown because we're unguarded (1 Corinthians 10:12). "What can we do?" we ask.

We can guard our relationship with God. As Proverbs 4:23 says,

> Above all else, guard your heart,
> for it is the wellspring of life.

There's a close relationship between human sexuality and human spirituality; the two are inextricably linked. As Charles Williams noted, "Sensuality and sanctity are so closely intertwined that our motives in some cases can hardly be separated until the tares are gathered out of the wheat by heavenly wit."

Sexual passion is in some inexplicable way a small representation of our more profound, spiritual passion for God. He alone can gratify that desire.

So devotion to Christ serves to satisfy our deepest longings and quell our other lusts. But when our love for Christ is on the wane, we get restless for something more, and our resolve in every area begins to weaken.

We can guard our minds against romantic and sexual fantasies. "Our predominant thoughts determine our inevitable actions," as someone has said. What we think in our hearts is what we eventually do. Most moral failures aren't blowouts (hardly anyone plans an adulterous affair) but are rather like slow leaks—the result of a thousand small indulgences, the immediate consequences of which are never apparent. The small sins thus prepare us for the Big One. As Alexander Pope remarked,

> Vice is a monster of so frightful mien,
>   As to be hated needs to be seen;
> Yet seen too often, familiar with her face,
>   We first endure, then pity, then embrace.

"But," you ask, "how can we deal with our erotic thoughts?" As Philip Melanchthon learned, "Old Adam is much too strong for young Philip!" I agree. Our fantasies are much too strong to subordinate. Better to rechannel or displace them. Erotic thoughts happen, but they can be controlled. As Luther said, "We cannot keep birds from flying over our heads, but we can keep them from nesting in our hair!" When sexual fantasies intrude into our minds, we have two choices: We can either reinforce them, in which case they will eventually become obsession; or we can sidetrack them into devotion, meditation, and prayer (see Philippians 4:8).

We men can give ourselves to being one-woman men. That's protection for both us and our spouses (see Proverbs 5:15–16). As the Wise Man counseled, we should "rejoice in the wife of [our] youth" and "be captivated by her love" (5:18–19). We can work hard at cultivating intimacy in our marriages—maintaining its romance, rekindling its love and passion. Men who get in trouble usually do so because they've let their marriages drift, permitting them to become dull and unfriendly. If that's so, we must woo our wives again, recapture our first love.

All of us—men and women—can watch for infatuations. In his *Introduction to the Devout Life*, Saint Francis de Sales said, "We must be on guard against deception in friendships, especially when they are contracted between persons of different sexes, no matter what the pretext may be. Satan often tricks those [who] begin with virtuous love. If they are not very prudent, fond love will first be injected, next sensual love, and then carnal love . . . [Satan] does this subtly and tries to introduce impurity by insensible degrees."

It's not lust but infatuation that causes our fall. Do we think about one person frequently? Do we look for excuses to be with that individual? Do we look forward to appointments with that one? Do we dress a certain way for him or her? Most erotic relationships begin with that subtle attraction. If we find ourselves drawn to another, we must go no further, not lunch nor travel nor time alone. When required to meet for business, we can do so in the company of others.

We can guard against intimacy with anyone other than our spouses. The secrets of our hearts, our deepest hurts, are reserved for our mates alone. The greatest mistake we can make is to share our inner conflict and marital disappointment with someone of the opposite sex. No other event so radically shifts the nature of a relationship. We suddenly become a lonely person in need of another person's love.

Occasionally a man will meet a woman who comes after him, as the proverb puts it, dressed for the kill and "with crafty intent" (7:10). And women are endangered by those sexual conquistadors who will tell them anything they want to hear in order to have what they want. We shouldn't kid ourselves. It's not because we're so wonderful that they love us. Such people live to bring others down; they have something to prove to themselves, or they want to see how much we'll forsake to have them. They're almost certainly acting out some terrible, inner sickness or playing out some unresolved conflict with the opposite sex. The best course is to stay away from them! It will do us good now and then to ponder well Proverbs 5 and 7.

We can publicize our home life, talk lovingly of our mates, and surround ourselves with mementos and reminders of our marriages—pictures of our families together. It's good for us, and it's good for others. It lets them know we cherish our homes.

We can regularly rehearse the consequences of an affair by asking ourselves, "Is it worth throwing away my family and my reputation for this event?"

We gain insight through hindsight, as they say, but foresight is the least expensive way to learn. As Proverbs 5:3–5 warns, though,

> the lips of an adulteress drip honey,
> and her speech is smoother than oil;

> [make no mistake] in the end she is bitter as gall,
>> sharp as a double-edged sword.
> Her feet go down to death;
>> her steps lead straight to the grave.

Adultery is suicidal; adulterers kill their own souls.

We can find someone who will hold us accountable—a nonjudgmental friend who loves us and who won't flinch when we're honest, who will query us with the tough questions and then ask, as Howard Hendricks suggests, "In your answers to any of the above, did you lie?"

And finally we can ask to be guarded by God every moment of the day. We're never safe. We're in danger whether young or old, single or married, in the dumps or on a roll. We'll never be home free until we get Home! Until then, no matter how willing the spirit, the flesh is weak. Jesus warned, "Watch and pray so that you will not fall into temptation" (Matthew 26:41).

—*A Burden Shared*

Hardships of Marriage

When the Lord saw that Leah was not loved, he opened her womb,
but Rachel was barren. Leah became pregnant and gave birth to
a son. She named him Reuben, for she said, "It is because the Lord
has seen my misery. Surely my husband will love me now."
—Genesis 29:31–32

Despite the assurance of countless fairy tales, there's no direct causal relationship between getting married and living happily ever after. Things go wrong—and sometimes terribly wrong. Despite the best of intentions, we may find ourselves in a house full of resentment, hostility, unrest, and misery. There is no heartache quite like that of an unhappy marriage.

Consider Jacob, who married well but soon saw domestic tranquility deteriorate into bickering, bitterness, and hatred. His dysfunctional household tore his heart to shreds. Yet Jacob's difficult marriage to Leah was just another phase of his spiritual formation, for God uses everything, even flawed and failed marriages, to get His hands on us and shape us into the men and women He has envisioned.

Some find family life to be their source of greatest satisfaction. Others find that its reversals, torments, and puzzles lead them to contemplate the meaning of life for the first time. A challenging marital relationship can be our schoolhouse, the means by which we become conformed to His will, until we are finally living in, by, and for Him alone.

Indeed, I know of no one who has entered into intimacy with God who has not at one time or another lost something thought to be indispensable. "What an ordinary person sees as necessary to have, God may take away from a person He is purifying," noted the seventeenth-century theologian Fenelon. And quite often it is the love of one's life.

It's only when other loves grow cold and still that we can begin to hear God's still, small voice whispering His love. It's when we lose the love we are sure we cannot do without that God gives us a love we cannot lose. As John Bunyan's Christian in *The Pilgrim's Progress* retorted to Obstinate, his detractor, "All that you forsake is not worthy to be compared with a little of what I am seeking to enjoy."

God often puts us into situations that seem to frustrate every hope of life, progress, and growth. Someone with much love to give finds herself in a marriage in which that love is unrequited. Another longs to bring peace to his home, yet lives in an atmosphere of unrelenting unrest, clamor, and confusion. The circumstances seem so meaningless and the efforts futile and impossibly difficult. Yet God knows exactly what He's doing. We must trust Him and submit to His will without struggling to escape. We only make life more painful for others and ourselves when we resist His hand. As Amy Carmichael put it, "In acceptance lieth peace."

This is not to say that we must accept physical, sexual, or emotional abuse or situations that endanger our children or ourselves. There are legitimate biblical bases for separation and divorce, although it's not my purpose to discuss them here. Suffice it to say that adversity does not in and of itself constitute a reason to break free. We must remain yielded, waiting for God's shaping and knowing all the while that He loves us deeply.

> The Lord's unfailing love
>   surrounds the [one] who trusts in him (Psalm 32:10).

No one could love us more. The comfort that comes from knowing we are held close in this kind of love is inexhaustible.

A difficult marriage provides a setting in which God can confront us with our skewed sense of self-importance. We begin to see ourselves for who we really are—not nearly as thoughtful, patient, polite, gracious, giving, and self-controlled as we have imagined ourselves to be. At best, marriage challenges these flattering illusions; at worst, it shatters them. We come to see how incurably ruined we are. Indifference, harshness, and coldness are the crosses on which our self-love begins to die.

We don't know to what extent Jacob's difficult marriage drew him toward God. Perhaps, at this stage of his life, not at all. But we do see in Leah's story a poignant vignette—a snapshot of one who in her suffering found herself in God. Unattractive and foisted on a husband who neither loved her nor wanted her, Leah pined for a love that never came. Few stories are more moving than her secret history and the profound heartache revealed in the names she gave her sons (Genesis 29:31–35).

She gave birth to her first son and named him Reuben ("Seen"), for she reasoned, "The Lord has seen my misery. Surely my husband will love me now." But he didn't.

Leah conceived again and gave birth to a son whom she named Simeon ("Heard"), "because the Lord heard that I am not loved." But Jacob still did not love her.

Again she conceived and gave birth to Levi ("Attached"), for "now at last my husband will become attached to me." But he didn't.

Leah conceived again and gave birth to Judah ("Praise"), vowing, "This time I will praise the Lord."

Jacob never loved Leah, but her longing for love was as satisfied as it can be in this life, for she had God and His perfect love. Oh, I'm certain she had times of great loneliness and days when her heart yearned for human love. Yet God was always there to comfort her, for God in time

> satisfies the thirsty
> and fills the hungry with good things (Psalm 107:9).

We're made for love—to love and be loved. But what of those whose love is never requited by a spouse? Must they wither away in loneliness and despair? No, they can still know perfect love and satisfaction, for God's love endures forever.

This is not to say that God will banish all our pain in this life, but our pain can lead us into a deeper love—the love of God—and greater fulfillment than we ever thought possible. And on ahead lies heaven where our joy will be complete.

If you are among the ranks of the unloved in this life, don't run from your pain or try to manufacture or manipulate love. Instead, give yourself to knowing God and loving Him. Let your deep need for affection and caring draw you into His heart. "He gives a greater grace"—greater than anything you could ever gain on your own.

And here is multiplied grace: When we find ourselves enveloped in God's love, we are free to give ourselves in simple, pure love—even to the one who has caused our pain.

I'm haunted by a story about F. B. Meyer, whose writings always encourage and enlighten me. Meyer once confided to a friend that he felt welcome in any home in England but his own. His loveless marriage was a source of deep heartache for him, yet Meyer believed that he, through his aching soul, was being prepared by God to give love and strength to others—and especially to his wife at the end of her days. He wrote to her:

> If then your future life should need
>   A strength my love can only gain
> Through suffering—or my heart be freed
>   Only by sorrow from some stain,
> Then you shall give, and I will take
>   This crown of fire for Love's dear sake.

Ignore the voices that tell you to set yourself free. They are nothing more than the echoes of self-love and will only lead you to greater emptiness and misery. "Remain," as the apostle Paul urges in 1 Corinthians 7:20. God is working through your heartache, working against your intentions and desires, but pressing you in His direction, holding you with His affection, molding you to His perfect design. There is no greater love.

—Jacob

Being a Godly Parent

Teach us how to bring up the boy who is to be born.
—Judges 13:8

This prayer of Manoah is the earnest and often anxious prayer of every godly parent.

The boy was Samson, Israel's prankish Hercules, who squandered his God-given strength. One wonders how often Manoah and his wife awakened in the dark, sleepless hours of the night and asked themselves, "Where did we go wrong?"

When our children make bad choices—when they abuse alcohol, do drugs, get pregnant out of wedlock, drop out of school, turn their backs on God and family—we ask ourselves the same question. We blame ourselves and see our children as the tragic victims of our ineptitude.

There is, however, no absolute correlation between the ways we parent and the way our children turn out. Good parenting makes a difference, but it does not guarantee that the product of that parenting will be good.

We all are acquainted with families where neglect, violence, and substance abuse are the norm, yet the children turn out remarkably well. They have good friends; they do well in school; they hold good jobs; they end up in stable marriages; and they handle their own parental responsibilities with wisdom and love. And we all are familiar with families where the parents are warm, nurturing, kind, firm, wise, and giving—and yet there's at least one prodigal in the family and sometimes more than one.

Despite our best efforts, our children may go wrong.

But, you say, what about Proverbs 22:6?

> Train a child in the way he should go,
> and when he is old he will not turn from it.

That sounds very much like a guarantee.

We must remember, however, that the biblical proverbs are not promises, but *premises*—general rules or axioms. Proverbs 22:6 is a statement of general truth, much like our contemporary saying: "As the twig is bent, so the tree is inclined." A proverb is a saying that sets forth a truth that is applicable in most cases, but there are always exceptions to the rule.

Why these exceptions? Because children are not mindless matter that we can shape at will. They are autonomous individuals who may, with the best of parenting, choose to go their own way. Even God, the perfect parent, has always had trouble with His children—Adam and Eve to name two. (You and me to name two more.)

If we believe that by applying certain techniques and rules we can secure godly behavior in our children, we may be in for bitter disillusionment and heartache. No one can determine or predict what his or her offspring will do.

Joaquin Andujar, poet and pitcher for the St. Louis Cardinals, said you could sum up baseball in one word: "You never know." His word count was off, but he captured the essence of life as well as baseball.

Given that uncertainty, the question is not "How can I produce godly children?" but rather "How can I be a godly parent?" The two questions may appear to be the same, but they're not. The first has to do with result, over which we have no control; the second with process, over which we do, by God's grace, have some measure of control.

If our focus is on process, then the questions are about us: How can I deal with my impatience, temper and rage, my selfishness, my resentment, my stubbornness, my defensiveness, my pride, my laziness, my unwillingness to listen? How can I deal with my addictions? How can I strengthen my marriage? How can I develop my parenting skills? How can I build bridges of grace, forgiveness, and acceptance that will make it possible for my prodigal to come home?

These are the matters that must occupy us as parents . . . and then we must leave the results with God.[6]

Ruth Bell Graham expressed it well:

> Lord, I will straighten all I can and You
> take over what we mothers cannot do.
>
> *—Out of the Ordinary*

---

6.   I am greatly indebted to Dr. John White and his book *Parents in Pain* for some of the ideas in this essay.

My Wish for All . . .

Moses replied, "Are you jealous for my sake?
I wish that all the Lord's people were prophets and that the
Lord would put his Spirit on them!"
—Numbers 11:29

Moses lamented: "I cannot carry all these people by myself; the burden is too heavy for me." God, who fully understood Moses' weariness, gathered Israel before the tabernacle. There He took some of the Spirit that was on Moses and put that Spirit on seventy of the elders of Israel (Numbers 11:14, 16–17). Each worker was filled and flooded with the fullness of the invisible God.

Then the Spirit broke forth. Sixty-eight of the seventy elders prophesied for a time and then ceased. But two continued to prophesy.

A young man ran and told Moses, "Eldad and Medad are prophesying in the camp." And Joshua, equally jealous for Moses' honor, added his sentiment: "Moses, my lord, stop them!" (11:27–28).

"Are you jealous for my sake?" Moses replied. "I wish that all the Lord's people were prophets and that the Lord would put his Spirit on them!"

This one remark establishes the greatness of Moses.

Little souls are addicted to their own significance. They're annoyed when others gain prominence, for they, like Diotrephes, "love to be first" (3 John 9). They seek greatness for themselves, though in time this always has the opposite effect. In Dante's *Inferno*, the poet's vision of hell, he portrays those who have esteemed themselves more highly than others carrying boulders on their shoulders that bend them double so they can only look at the ground, for on earth they always looked down on others.

Those who exhibit enduring greatness delight in seeing others use their gifts; they are content to decrease if others increase. They serve the glory of Christ and the good of His people. They have no greater joy than to hear that their children walk in truth and are surpassing them.

There is no more searching test than this: Am I as eager for God's kingdom to come through others as I am for it to come through me?

I ask myself: Do I take joy in the success of others, even my "competition" (Philippians 1:18)? Can I pray for and encourage younger, more gifted men and women who take my place? Can I esteem them more highly than I do myself (Philippians 2:3)? Am I willing to be anything (or nothing) if God's eternal purposes are served?

I cannot ask these questions without feeling shame, for they expose the selfish ambition that is mingled with all other motives. Oh, that you and I could say with Moses, "I wish that *all* the Lord's people were prophets and that the Lord would put his Spirit on them," and rejoice in *their* joy when they're honored and exalted beyond us.

"Let us know how to sit, as well as how to rise," wrote John Wesley, "and let it comfort our declining days to trace, in those who are likely to succeed us in our work, the openings of yet greater usefulness."

This spirit can only grow in us as we are taken into God's great heart and see His passion to be glorified in *all* His saints (2 Thessalonians 1:10). There we learn to care more for *His* work than for our own.

If I would do great things, "I must decrease" (John 3:30 NASB).

—Out of the Ordinary

When in Doubt . . .

Rehoboam rejected the advice the elders gave him and consulted
[instead] the young men who had grown up with him.
—1 Kings 12:8

Jake was old. His legs were thin and bowed; they seemed much too spindly to hold him against the current of the Deschutes River. His waders looked older still: They were discolored, cracked, and patched. His fishing vest was jerry-rigged with safety pins; his ancient cowboy hat was battered and sweat-stained. His antiquated fiberglass fly rod was scarred and taped. He was hardly state-of-the-art.

I watched bemused as he worked his way upstream into a patch of quiet water and began to cast. And then I really took notice! He was fishing water I'd fished earlier, putting his fly over pockets I'd missed, taking trout where I'd caught none. Here was a man who could teach me a thing or two! Emerson was right: "Every man is my superior in some way. In that I can learn from him."

And so I ask myself, "Where can I find some old-timer who is my superior in the Word, who knows God as I want to know Him; where is that spiritual director and counselor in whom I can find security?"

They're somewhat uncommon, but they are surely there and we must find them. God leaves none of us without witness. Everyone can teach us a little, but occasionally there are older, wiser souls in whom we can trust and from whom we can learn much. These sages are our safety. We've got to find them, cultivate their friendship, and hear what they have to say.

As Thomas à Kempis said, "Who is so wise as to be able to know all things? Therefore, trust not too much in your own thoughts, but be willing also to

165

hear the sentiments of others . . . It is more safe to hear and take counsel than to give it. It may happen that one's thought may be good; but to refuse to yield to others, when reason or just cause requires it, is a sign of pride and willfulness."

The ability to listen to one's elders is unnatural, but it's a quality that has to be learned, and sometimes it's learned the hard way.

I think of Rehoboam, Solomon's son and the successor to his throne. You would expect some of Solomon's famous wisdom to have rubbed off on the young man, but unfortunately, as Solomon aged and edged away from God, the old king made a fool of himself.

One of his worst mistakes was to conscript Israelites as slave labor to build "the Lord's temple, his own palace, the supporting terraces, the wall of Jerusalem, and Hazor, Megiddo and Gezer . . . He built up Lower Beth Horon, Baalath, and Tadmor . . . as well as all his store cities and the towns for his chariots and for his horses" (1 Kings 9:15–19).

It would have been one thing to build a national sanctuary—an exceptional work that would have galvanized his people and enlisted their sympathies—but it was another to coerce them into building projects that served only to aggrandize the king. That unwelcome chore created widespread dissatisfaction and several times brought Israel to the edge of civil war. So when Solomon died and a new order emerged, the tribes from the north and their would-be leader, Jeroboam, appealed to Rehoboam for relief: "Your father put a heavy yoke on us, but now lighten the harsh labor . . . and we will serve you" (12:4).

Rehoboam was nonplussed. He asked for time to consider their request and then consulted the elders who had served his father: " 'How would you advise me to answer these people?' he asked. They replied, 'If today you will be a servant to these people and serve them and give them a favorable answer, they will always be your servants' " (12:6–7).

The elders gave sound advice—good leaders should lead by compassion and not by fear—but Rehoboam "rejected the advice the elders gave him and consulted [instead] the young men who had grown up with him and were serving him. He asked them, 'What is your advice? How should we answer these people?' " The young men replied, "Tell them, 'My little finger is thicker than my father's waist. My father laid on you a heavy yoke; I will make it even heavier. My father scourged you with whips; I will scourge you with scorpions [a type of whip with iron hooks]' " (12:10–11).

And so, taking the counsel of his young friends, Rehoboam began his reign by cracking his whip, but his gambit failed. Jeroboam and his followers walked out, and Israel seceded from Judah and crowned Jeroboam as their king. Rehoboam had single-handedly torn the nation apart—a schism from which they never recovered—all because he forsook the advice of his elders and listened instead to his peers.

As I thought about this foolishness, a principle emerged: When in doubt, ask an old grizzly. All of us need the counsel of older, wiser folks. (In my case it's time for me to find an even older grizzly.)

Of course not all old-timers are wise. There are wise old folks and there are wicked old folks, and some men and women just get to be old fools. But since all knowledge, wisdom, and character is cumulative, it follows that those who have loved the Savior a long time will reach maturity rich in their understanding of God and be wise in His ways. Think of the calm He brings, the understanding He leaves them, "the hoarded spoils, the legacies of time."

Old-timers who have walked a long time with God and have listened well to His counsel usually have something to say. It's good to seek them out and heed their counsel. In a multitude of such counselors, there is safety (Proverbs 11:14).

—*A Burden Shared*

A Man of Few Words

When words are many, sin is not absent.
—Proverbs 10:19

It's wise to be brief, to say as little as possible to others and as much as possible to God. "Many words are meaningless" (Ecclesiastes 5:7).

Too much talk weakens our character. It's like the continuous running of a faucet that empties a well. Talking leaves no time to commune with ourselves and with God.

"Silence is the mother of the wisest thoughts," said Diadochus, an early Christian writer. Our thoughts mature in quiet moments. If we're always talking, we give no opportunity for our hearts to receive the promptings of the Spirit; we can't hear what others are saying, and we can't hear what the Spirit wants us to say.

Furthermore, we can't be talking all the time without saying things that cause us regret. We talk too much about ourselves or too much about others. Our words coerce, contaminate, and offend our friends.

How often have I walked away from meetings with a bad taste in my mouth (could it be my foot?) thinking, *I should have left some things unsaid.*

"When words are many, sin is not absent" (Proverbs 10:19)—a verse that Augustine said "frightens me a great deal." It frightens me a great deal as well.

> Do you see a man who speaks in haste?
> There is more hope for a fool than for him (Proverbs 29:20).

The one who is hasty—who always has to say something—usually doesn't consult God at all. He already knows what's best for any situation. He can act on his own. "Such a man," said Fenelon, "is the greatest fool in the world."

How often I have played the fool by being much too chatty. I must learn to be silent before God—set the door of my heart wide open, back to the wall—and ask Him to fill me with His words and His wisdom. It's in silence that God will give me something to say. He will teach me to speak—or not to speak.

Isaiah said of our Lord,

> He will delight in the fear of the Lord.
> He will not judge by what he sees with his eyes,
>   or decide by what he hears with his ears (11:3).

Jesus heard and saw many things, but He never uttered a word on His own. He said of Himself, "Whatever I say is just what the Father has told me to say" (John 12:50).

When the Pharisees came to Jesus with the woman caught in adultery, He did not reply to their question immediately but knelt for a moment and scribbled something in the sand. I have no idea what He wrote, but I think I know what He was doing: He was waiting to hear from His Father.

When He finally spoke, it was one short sentence: "If any one of you is without sin, let him be the first to throw a stone at her" (John 8:7). Those few words accomplished more than any self-derived sermon would have achieved. Even today those words resound around the world. We must stop and think before we speak, but more to the point, we must stop and pray.

I think of Vincent van Gogh's illustration of a quiet, inviting cottage beside the road. There's a warm fire inside that no one can see, but wisps of smoke come out of the chimney. Someone inside is tending the fire, waiting patiently for the hour when some traveler will come by and sit down, maybe to talk, maybe to stay. Silence toward others and openness toward God enable us to tend that fire.

James says we must be "quick to listen [to what God has to say]" and "slow to speak" (James 1:19). This is not the slowness of ignorance, emptiness, timidity, guilt, or shame. This is the slowness of wisdom born of dwelling quietly with God.

—In Quietness and Confidence

Healed So We Can Heal

I served the Lord with great humility and with tears.
—Acts 20:19

I'll never forget a funeral I conducted for a small child. As we waited for the family to gather, a little boy walked up to the tiny casket and gazed in. He was obviously distressed, and I wanted to comfort him. "Your little sister is with Jesus," I said. Good theology. Bad timing.

He burst into tears. "I don't want her to be with Jesus," he sobbed, "I want her here with me so we can play!" I put my arm around him and we both cried.

Sometimes tears are the only thing we can do for another, the only thing we should do. As George MacDonald discovered, "Tears are often the only cure for weeping."

Christians aren't Stoics, striving to be pure mind without passion. Stoicism is a dehumanizing, pagan ethic; there's nothing Christian about it. It confuses discipline with suppression, reduces self-control to the repression of all emotion, and curbs all feelings in their outward expression.

Jesus' example instructs us otherwise. There was no embarrassment in His grief. When confronted with suffering, "Jesus wept" (John 11:35).

Talking is what I usually do. It's what I'm paid to do. But sometimes there are simply no words to say. I sit in silence and wait. But when words are most empty, tears are most apt. Our compassion can relieve those who suffer from the worst misery of all—the feeling of being alone in their misery. Much can be said without anything being spoken.

That kind of compassion can't be generated, but it can grow on us. Being around people helps. We can't be with them very long without becoming aware of their longings and hurts. Our kinship links us to their sorrows.

Compassion also grows out of our own failure and sin. Unjudged sin can harden us and separate us from others, but sin acknowledged and repented of sensitizes us to others' frailty and draws us closer to them. Common sin is our common ground; publicans and sinners become our kind of people.

Compassion likewise grows through our own suffering. Paul reminds us that God is the source of mercy and comfort who comforts us in all our afflictions so we can comfort others. "If we are distressed," he wrote, "it is for your comfort and salvation" (2 Corinthians 1:6). Personal pain is a prerequisite for consoling others. As A. W. Tozer said, "It's doubtful that God can use any man greatly until he's been hurt deeply."

We all have our own particular sorrows. Our wounds are not always scratches; sometimes they're deep and ugly and near-mortal. But God cares and cures. When earthly comforts fail us, He gives "eternal encouragement" (2 Thessalonians 2:16). Pain moves us closer to our Father, and we gain His perspective on our broken dreams; we get His comfort; "by his wounds we are healed" (Isaiah 53:5).

But we get more than salve for our own wounds: We are healed so we can heal. We're made more human and humane, more kind and empathetic. We understand and our understanding helps people. Thus, by our wounds others are healed.

And finally, compassion comes from worship and prayer. Compassion is ultimately a gift from God. More seminars than ever aim to make us sensitive to others, but true compassion can never be the product of systematic study or effort. It is the fruit of intimacy with the God who cares for us (1 Peter 5:7).

His caring begets caring for others. His compassion rubs off on us; His love becomes ours. Our love by Love grows mighty in His love.

—*A Burden Shared*

Wanting to Run Away

Oh, that I had in the desert
a lodging place for travelers,
so that I might leave my people
and go away from them.
—Jeremiah 9:2

Sometimes I think Jeremiah had it exactly right. He wanted a cabin in the woods where he could get away from it all. He was fed up with folks; he'd had it. He wanted out—way out—away from them all.

I get the feeling myself from time to time—the yen to get a job in a lighthouse or drop out and build a log cabin with my own hands way up in the mountains and let the world go to pieces. Deep down I just want to be left alone.

It's a pervasive fantasy. William Yeats felt the urge:

> I will arise now and go to Innisfree . . .
> And live alone in the bee-loud glade.

King David did too: "Oh, that I had the wings of a dove!" he cried.

> I would fly away and be at rest—
> I would flee far away
>   and stay in the desert;
> I would hurry to my place of shelter,
>   far from the tempest and storm (Psalm 55:6–8).

I think everybody must get that inclination now and then. Genesis says that it's not good to be alone, but honestly sometimes being alone sounds like the best thing in the world.

I get tired of the hassles, the responsibilities, the everlasting demands, the wall-to-wall people. There is no end of things to be done for others. I get weary of doing things for them and hearing about their worries and woes.

It's then that I begin to dream about dropping out and going away.

But it won't do. Final escape is a fantasy, and fantasy has no place in our lives. We're to be girded about with reality (Ephesians 6:14).

We can't drop out. There's more at stake than our own solace.

That's why the word came to Jeremiah from the Lord: "Proclaim all these words in the *towns* of Judah and in the *streets* of Jerusalem. 'Listen to the terms of this covenant and follow them' " (Jeremiah 11:6).

Jeremiah couldn't stay in the high country; he had to go back to town. There were things to be done, the word to be proclaimed, people to be helped on to God.

Raphael's altarpiece in the Vatican depicts Jesus on the Mountain of Transfiguration with the three disciples, James, Peter, and John. All is light and glory. At the foot of the mountain all is gloom and doom. The disciples want to remain on the mountaintop, but Jesus won't let them stay. They have to come down with Him and live in the world of darkness and demons, down where the redemptive rubber meets the road.

It's necessary to go to the mountains and get away now and then; William Blake said,

> Great things are done when men and mountains meet;
> This is not done by jostling in the street.

We should by all means find some time to be alone and get away from the crowds, if only for a few hours each week. We need a quiet place in which to rest and in which God can recreate our love for Him and refresh our souls. The mountain renews us as it renewed our Lord. He often went into the mountains so there would be nothing between Him and God (see Luke 6:12).

Though solitude is a good place to visit, it's no place to stay. God says to us what he said to Jeremiah, "Proclaim all these words in the *towns* . . . and in the *streets*."

—*A Burden Shared*

The Right Place at the Right Time—
To Minister Even to One

Then the word of the Lord came to him: "Go at once to Zarephath
of Sidon and stay there. I have commanded a widow in that place
to supply you with food." So he went to Zarephath.
—1 Kings 17:8–10

Here's the remarkable thing: Elijah, Israel's great prophet, was not sent to square off with the king of Sidon but to board with a solitary widow in the little town of Zarephath. She was a Canaanite, a fact so offensive to the ancient rabbis that they contrived to represent her as a disenfranchised Jew and made her out to be the mother of Jonah. But it wasn't so. She wasn't a child of the covenant. She was a raw pagan.

It seems odd to us that God would send his great representative across Israel to Phoenicia to find a solitary woman and draw her in. But that's the way He is. He is not willing that any should perish. He loves all people, great and small.

I never read the story of Elijah and the widow in Zarephath without thinking of Jesus' foray to this very region. The two narratives are strikingly similar.

Jesus had withdrawn from Israel into Phoenicia, as Elijah did, to the coast near the city of Tyre. He rented a house there and settled down. By that time Phoenicia had lost much of her greatness, but her fierce pride and immorality remained. It was a hotbed of hostility to God.

Mark reported that a certain woman intruded into their all-male reverie. "Lord, Son of David, have mercy on me" (Matthew 15:22), she blurted out.

She had a severely tormented child. She termed her daughter "terribly" demonized.

Matthew described her as Canaanite, part of the native population. Mark added additionally that she was a Greek by religion. We think of the Greeks as cultured and refined, and they were—yet their religion was essentially Devil worship. Their word for divinity, *daimonion*, is the word from which we get our word "demon," and Paul clearly stated that those who worshiped the Greek gods of his day were actually worshiping the Devil.

Perhaps this woman introduced her daughter to practices that led to her infestation. Her mother's heart was broken for her daughter—and for her own shame.

She made a terrible pest of herself—wouldn't take no for a negative. Her cries were persistent and pathetic, but strangely, Jesus ignored her. That's so unlike our Lord, whose ears are always attentive to our cries.

His delay was for His disciples, whose racism and sexism had broken His heart. He tested them by saying, "I was sent only to the lost sheep of Israel" (Matthew 15:24). His disciples would have quickly agreed, disinclined as they were to believe that one like this woman could ever care about God.

But she did care about God. She had heard Him calling from afar. She was one of God's lost sheep, whom Jesus said are "not of this sheep pen," but who "will listen to [his] voice" (John 10:16). This was a lesson in finding one errant sheep wherever it happened to be. Here in the story of the Syrophoenician woman we have another glimpse of the seeking, calling Shepherd: All are precious in His sight.

Jesus said to her, "First let the children eat" (Mark 7:27). The children, of course, were the children of God. Feeding them was Jesus' ministry.

"It is not right to take the children's bread and toss it to their dogs," Jesus said.

"Yes, Lord," she replied, perhaps with a twinkle in her eyes, "but even the [puppies] eat the crumbs that fall from their masters' table" (Matthew 15:27).

She had her eyes on her Master. *I may be a puppy,* she mused, *but I'm your puppy. Puppies have their rights.*

What audacious wit! "Was not that a master-stroke?" Luther said. "She snares Christ in His own words."

Jesus said to the woman, "You have great faith!" (15:28). There were only two people in the world to whom He made that statement: a Roman centurion and this Canaanite. Both were outsiders.

"When the Son of Man comes, will he find faith on the earth?" Jesus asked (Luke 18:8). Yes indeed—in the most unlikely places and in the most unlikely people. He will find faith in those parts of our culture where men and women are tired of doing evil—and where even the good things of life no longer satisfy. Hopeless, they come seeking tenderness.

And God meets them!

It is His own decision, based on His choice, to pour out His love. He is driven by love, not by their attractiveness. He is drawn to them—even (and especially) those who have done everything wrong.

"What do you think?" said Jesus. "If a man owns a hundred sheep, and one of them wanders away, will he not leave the ninety-nine on the hills and go to look for the one that wandered off? And if he finds it, I tell you the truth, he is happier about that one sheep than about the ninety-nine that did not wander off. In the same way your Father in heaven is not willing that any of these little ones should be lost" (Matthew 18:12–14).

Lost sheep are not doomed; they're the ones He came to save. "The ambitious, the vain, the highly sexed," said C. H. Sisson, are Christ's "natural prey."

There was a plaque that used to hang over my mother's desk. I saw it every day. It used to get under my skin, but then—it finally worked its way into my heart: "Only one life, 'twill soon be past. Only what's done for Christ will last."

John Wesley said to his young Methodists, "You have nothing to do but to save souls. Therefore spend and be spent in this work . . . It is not your main business . . . to take care of this or that society; but to save as many souls as you can; to bring as many sinners as you possibly can to repentance, and with all your power to build them up in that holiness without which they cannot see the Lord."

We must be faithful where we are—befriending one or two, if that's all we can do, loving them and imparting God's truth to them. As Francis Schaeffer used to say, "There are no little places and there are no little people." Every person in every place is of infinite value to God. "If there were only one of us," Augustine said, "Jesus would still have died."

"Who despises the day of small things?" asked one of Haggai's contemporaries (Zechariah 4:10). The answer, of course, is that we do. *Small* has fallen on hard times, inclined as we are to equate size with success. Small is now a value judgment: If we're limited to one or two, we're hardly worth anything at all.

Some years ago when I was involved in a ministry to university students, I invited a prominent Christian speaker to address a group of students on our campus. When only one person showed up, he refused to talk to her. He was too big to speak to a crowd that small.

Some people look good with the masses but fail miserably when it comes to one or two. Yet our love for one person is the test of our love for all. Authentic Christianity is this: "to look after orphans and widows in their distress" (James 1:27). Reality reveals itself in quiet acts of mercy and goodness that no one sees or applauds—but God.

Think of our Lord—His lofty mission to save the world and yet His lowly manner. He always had time for one soul. Take Zacchaeus, for example. Zacchaeus had sold out to the evil empire and in the eyes of his own people had bartered his soul to the Devil. He had forsaken the way of the law and was on his way to gehenna. If he were in business today, he would be trafficking in illegal drugs or kiddie porn, but his heart was clambering for God.

No one took him seriously.

Except Jesus.

He knew the little man was looking for something.

Jesus picked Zacchaeus out of the crowd and invited Himself over for lunch. "'Zacchaeus, come down immediately. I must stay at your house today.' So he came down at once and welcomed him gladly" (Luke 19:5–6). Jesus' self-invitation sounds presumptuous to us, but in His culture it was a gesture of acceptance. You ate and drank only with people you preferred. Zacchaeus knew that Jesus wanted to be his friend. And so it is. He was every sinner's friend: "The Son of Man came to seek and to save what was lost" (19:10).

Zacchaeus, when he heard Jesus' offer, came down out of his tree to sit with Him and listen to Him. Later he rose from the table to say, " 'Look, Lord! Here and now I give half of my possessions to the poor, and if I have cheated anybody out of anything, I will pay back four times the amount.' Jesus said to him, 'Today, salvation has come to this house, because this man, too, is a son of Abraham' " (19:8–9).

Zacchaeus had been brought in. The Son of Man had found one who was lost. He still has love for one person; He still sends His messengers after a single, solitary soul. As F. B. Meyer observed, "The mighty great cares about the mighty small."

One stormy Sunday Edward Payson, a famous preacher of a bygone era, had only one person in his audience. Payson preached his sermon as carefully and earnestly as though the building were filled with eager listeners.

Some months later his lone attendee called on him: "I was led to the Savior through that service," he said. "For whenever you talked about sin and salvation, I glanced around to see to whom you referred, but since there was no one there but me, I had no alternative but to lay every word to my heart and conscience!"

One or two is not too few; it's just about right. God saves people one by one. Size is nothing; substance is everything. So you only have access to one. *That* is your mission field. Saving one is not a stepping-stone to greatness. It is greatness. It's all a matter of perspective. We are not called upon to love the world and bring salvation to it. Only God "so loved the world." Our business, as Jesus made clear in the parable of the Good Samaritan, is to love our neighbors. "Who is my neighbor?" we ask. The next person we meet along the way whose deep needs God exposes to our eyes.

Our Lord did not have time to meet every need around Him. There were many lepers in Israel who never experienced His touch. There were many widows and orphans for whom He had no word. He did only what the Father told Him to do. He let God decide.

And so must we.

Ask God to bring you today to the one He has prepared. He will get you to the right place at the right time to speak to that person. He is prepared to dwell in your body, speak through your lips, work through your hands, and fulfill in you the great purpose of His will.

Carolyn and I were flying from Frankfurt, Germany, to our home in Boise, Idaho. The first leg was Frankfurt to Boston. It had been an exhausting week, and I dropped off to sleep as soon as I found my seat, but I was soon awakened by a disturbance in the aisle.

The steward and a passenger who had been seated on Carolyn's left were arguing about the man's seat assignment. Somehow he had been separated from his fiancée, who was seated several rows behind us.

The man grew increasingly angry until another passenger, seated by the man's fiancée, offered to trade places. The swap was made, and Carolyn's new seatmate settled into his place, drew out a legal pad, and began to work on some project.

But a garrulous French boy seated on his left—a charming child—wanted to talk. The man, who seemed to be the soul of patience, gave up his project after a few minutes to chat amiably with the boy. Carolyn was soon drawn into the conversation.

I heard the man say he was from Los Gatos, California, a town close to Los

Altos, where Carolyn and I had lived for eighteen years. He was on the first leg of a flight to San Francisco. I heard Carolyn say we had many friends in the Bay Area, and then I went back to sleep.

When I awakened an hour or so later, I found Carolyn sharing her faith with her newfound friend, scribbling on his pad of paper, drawing diagrams, and animating her story. He was listening intently and asking questions. I sat there quietly and prayed for her and for the man.

At one point he said, "You believe as my wife does."

"Oh?" Carolyn replied. "And how did she become a follower of Christ?"

"Through Bible Study Fellowship," he responded.

"How did she find out about Bible Study Fellowship?" Carolyn asked.

"A friend of hers, Nel King, invited her to attend."

"That's remarkable!" Carolyn exclaimed. "Nel King is one of my best friends!"

And then the coin dropped: A few months before we moved to Boise, Nel had asked Carolyn to pray for a friend who had just become a Christian through Bible Study Fellowship and for her husband who was not yet a believer—the man now seated on Carolyn's left—there "by that power which erring men call chance."

—Elijah

The Cure for Conflict

What causes fights and quarrels among you? Don't they come
from your desires that battle within you?
—James 4:1

Conflict, like death and taxes, is unavoidable. Nations rage, neighbors feud, siblings strive, lovers quarrel, and churches fight. One zigs, the other zags. Life is full of dissonance. What can we do?

One sure way to temporarily conciliate another is to lose—give in. And some would argue that humility and submission demand it. But God-fearing men and women aren't meant to be pushovers. They seek first the kingdom of God and His righteousness and not peace at any cost. "The wisdom that comes from heaven is *first of all* pure; then peace-loving" (James 3:17).

Furthermore, no one wins when one party always wins. Winning under those conditions is a wasted, Pyrrhic victory.

Antagonists can dig in and defend rigid (or shifting) positions and try to wear one another down by argument and contest of will, or one can pull rank and insist on surrender, but no one gets to agreement either way. As Samuel Butler said, "He that complies against his will is of the same opinion still."

When all else fails we can beat up on one another—verbally if not physically—like the lawyers who, when they found themselves on the short end of a debate with Jesus, resorted to name calling. ("We were not born of fornication," they cackled, clearly implying that He was [John 8:41 NKJV].)

Or we can do it James's peaceable way. Consider his counsel: "What causes fights and quarrels among you? Don't they come from your desires that battle within you? You want something but don't get it. You kill and covet, but you cannot have what you want. You quarrel and fight. You do not have, because you do not ask God. When you do ask, you do not receive, because you ask with wrong motives, that you may spend what you get on your pleasures" (James 4:1–3).

"What causes fights and quarrels?" Good question. James gets to the root of the problem. Conflict comes from our "desires," a word suggesting "something that satisfies." Underlying all conflict is this hidden factor—one's personal interest and longing for satisfaction.

People are bundles of needs, wants, hopes, dreams, fears, and ambitions that are doing battle within them, fighting for satisfaction. It's these cross-currents of personal concern that put us on the road to conflict with others. When the pursuit of our own interests is blocked by others' pursuits of their own interests, we become frustrated and conflict develops. (Consider, for example, what happens when Young Husband comes home seeking silence and solitude and encounters Young Wife, whose most intelligent conversation all day long has been with a two-year-old child!)

This is why arguments are almost never about the subject under debate. Underneath the conflict is the covert factor of personal concern. These concerns are the interests that motivate people; they are the silent movers behind the positions we take.

Therefore the first step in conflict resolution is temporarily to set aside the surface problems and the positions we've adopted and try to get in touch with one another's underlying concerns. As Paul said, "Each of you should look not only to your own interests, but also to the interests of others" (Philippians 2:4–5).

That takes a bit of doing. We have to peel away the outer layers of perceptions and emotions until we get to the heart. Ultimately the resolution of any conflict lies not in the conflict itself but in people's hearts.

And that means loving one another—putting ourselves in the others' shoes; trying to see the merits of their case. It means forgoing blame, not holding them responsible for the problem. It means sending "I" messages rather than "you" messages—talking about ourselves and how we feel rather than what the other has done. It means "believing all things," rather than putting the worst interpretation on what the other side says or does. It means refusing to pout or stonewall or walk out. It means apologizing when we get out of hand.

It means asking questions and listening actively and acknowledging what's being said, asking the other party to spell out carefully and clearly exactly what is meant, requesting that ideas be repeated if there is ambiguity or uncertainty, and repeating what we have heard the other person say, all of which can lead to understanding.

Once we understand one another's bottom-line concerns, we can begin to invent options for mutual gain, collaborating in a hardheaded, side-by-side search for solutions that will benefit both.

"But," you ask, "what if the other party won't dance and we're denied and left wanting?" (see James 4:2). For some that's an invitation to "quarrel and fight" and even to "kill." (Most killings are not premeditated but rather crimes of passion, deeply regretted after the fact.)

James has an unexpected answer: We should ask God to meet our needs His way (4:2–3). Rather than take matters into our own hands, it's far better to ask God to supply what we must have and to ask with sincerity— "Not my will but Yours be done."

It does no good to blame others or brood over our plight. Rather we should talk to the One who knows our deepest needs long before we become aware of them and who cares about us more than we can imagine. We can tell Him about our anger and hurt, our fears and frustration; He can handle any emotion. But we should then ask Him to meet our needs His way, for, as James would say, we should not ask "with wrong motives."

But when God meets our needs, "he gives us more grace" (4:6). Frustrated desire becomes an open door to more of God and an opportunity to have more of our needs met than we could ever imagine.

To satisfy our interests apart from God is a serious matter! Follow James's argument: "You adulterous people, don't you know that friendship with the world is hatred toward God? Anyone who chooses to be a friend of the world becomes an enemy of God. Or do you think Scripture says without reason that the spirit he caused to live in us envies intensely? But he gives us more grace. That is why Scripture says: 'God opposes the proud but gives grace to the humble' " (4:4–6).

God is like a jealous husband who longs to satisfy the deepest desires of His bride. All she has to do is ask. Perhaps He will give the very thing desired, or He may, out of infinite wisdom, substitute another, better thing, but His solutions are always the best solutions of all.

But when we fail to ask and insist on satisfying ourselves in ways other than His, we are like a wanton, adulterous wife who will not come to her mate with her needs. Or, to pick up on James's mixed metaphor, we've made friends with the world, since self-assertion, and not simple dependence on God, is the secular way of satisfying one's needs.

Since, therefore, we belong to a loving, caring Lord, we should

> submit . . . to God [since our circumstances are His will]. Resist the devil, and he will flee from you. [Though he would entice us to fight for self-interest at the expense of another, he has no defense against faith.] Come near to God and he will come near to you. [He responds lovingly and patiently to our needs.] Wash your hands, you sinners, and purify your hearts, you double-minded. Grieve, mourn and wail. [To insist upon our interests is a serious sin for it produces "disorder and every evil practice" (3:16).] Change your laughter to mourning and your joy to gloom. [Self-assertion is no laughing matter!] Humble yourselves before the Lord, and he will lift you up [an unequivocal promise!] (4:7–10).

Coming to a Father who delights in us and who gives us dignity is the added dimension that books on conflict resolution seem to miss. Perhaps their authors do not know God and do not know that He longs to give His children more than they could ever get on their own.

—*A Burden Shared*

The Telltale Tongue

The tongue also is a fire, a world of evil among the parts of the body. It corrupts the whole person, sets the whole course of his life on fire, and is itself set on fire by hell.

All kinds of animals, birds, reptiles and creatures of the sea are being tamed and have been tamed by man, but no man can tame the tongue. It is a restless evil, full of deadly poison.

With the tongue we praise our Lord and Father, and with it we curse men, who have been made in God's likeness. Out of the same mouth come praise and cursing. My brothers, this should not be.
—James 3:6–10

Nothing is easier than sinning, and there are many ways to sin, but mostly we sin by what we say. "How much must I be changed before I am changed?" as John Donne said.

Actually James goes beyond our words and looks deep down into our hearts. Not only do we sin by what we say, he insists, but what we say is the measure of our sinfulness: "If anyone is never at fault in what he says, he is a perfect man, able to keep his whole body in check" (James 3:2). "Stick out your tongue," says Dr. James. "I want to see the state of your soul." Thus James begins his treatise on the tongue.

The tongue is a little member, he observes, yet it can do great things. Three metaphors make his point: Little bits control strong horses; little rudders turn mighty sailing ships; little sparks ignite vast conflagrations. Little things mean a lot.

The tongue, though very small, "makes great boasts" (3:5). "Look what I can do," it struts and brags. "I can ruin a reputation. I can destroy a lifework.

I can rupture a long-standing relationship. I can crush the strongest spirit. I can spoil the tenderest moment. I can humiliate, embarrass, and shame. I can curse and cut and kill!"

"[The tongue]," says James, "corrupts the whole person, sets the whole course of his life on fire, and is itself set on fire by hell" (3:6). The tongue defiles every part of our being and every moment of our lives from the cradle to the grave. It burns its way through our "life cycle" to use James's exact expression, like an out-of-control forest fire, leaving devastation and ruin. Only in our death will it die.

James's word for hell is *gehenna,* Jerusalem's garbage dump, a fitting metaphor for hell in those days, associated as it was with impurity, corruption, fumes, and stench, a place ruled by Baal-zebub, the Lord of the Flies—the source of the filth that so readily rolls off our tongues.

And here's the worst of it: "You can tame a tiger," *The Message* says, "but you can't tame a tongue—it's never been done" (3:7–8). It is a restless, vicious, venomous, feral thing that cannot be controlled—at least by man.

Finally James notes an odd incongruity: With our tongues we bless God and curse men, the most god-like beings on earth. Blessings and curses from the same orifice. "My brothers," says James in a masterpiece of understatement, "this should not be" (3:10).

Who can explain this strange ambivalence? James's answer is to consider the source: "Does a fountain send out from the same opening both fresh and bitter water? Can a fig tree, my brethren, produce olives, or a vine produce figs? Neither can salt water produce fresh" (3:11–12 NASB).

Fresh water flows from fresh subterranean sources, bitter water from deep springs of bitterness. James doesn't explain his metaphor. He lets it hang in the air and leaves it for us to think through. That's the best thing you can do for another, George MacDonald said: "Wake things up that are in him; or make him think out things for himself."

Having thought about it for a while, here's what I believe James had in mind. Our words are formed deep within in our hearts. Good words come from the good in us; evil words flow from the evil we have accumulated within. If we want to deal with our tongues, we have to get our minds right.

Jesus put it in clear and concise language: "No good tree bears bad fruit, nor does a bad tree bear good fruit. Each tree is recognized by its own fruit. People do not pick figs from thorn bushes, or grapes from briers. The good man brings good things out of the good stored up in his heart, and the evil man brings evil things out of the evil stored up in his heart. For out of the overflow of his heart his mouth speaks" (Luke 6:43–45).

The heart is the storehouse of the body. We must be careful, then, of the things we put inside it. They can become words at any moment.

How can we get our words right? We must fill our thoughts with God's words—meditate on them day and night. The secret of good words is the Word of God, delighted in and meditated upon, for what is the Word of God but the life of God which always translates itself into human speech?

Let me illustrate how this works for me, at least in one situation (though I must say I don't always make it work). Certain folks "bring out the worst in me" (interesting phrase). I find it unnatural and, in some cases, impossible to curb my tongue when I'm around them. Like David, my heart grows hot within me, and as I meditate (here's that word again) the fire burns and I speak with my tongue (Psalm 39:3). At best I'm curt and discourteous; at worst I give them a "piece of my mind."

"Aha!" I say. The problem is not my words, you see, but my mind. Long before I open my mouth, I have opened my mind to wrong thinking. I have rehearsed the wrong done to me by my brother. I have nursed my hurt feelings. I have imputed wrong motives. I have pandered to self-pity and pride. I have harbored resentment and rage. "The fire burns and I speak with my tongue." My heated words have been created and shaped by my thoughts long before they spill out of my mouth. How can anything clean come from something unclean?

Paul says, "Whatever is true, whatever is noble, whatever is right, whatever is pure, whatever is lovely, whatever is admirable—if anything is excellent or praiseworthy—*think about such things*" (Philippians 4:8). He's not suggesting that I give myself to noble abstractions, as good as that may be, but rather that I focus on those attributes in others that are true, noble, righteous, pure, admirable, and lovable.

In other words, instead of obsessing over the wrong that I see in others, I must focus on the good God is doing in them. (Remember, it's not just Christians who have good things going for them. Every human being is a recipient of God's common grace.) When I do so, I see blessedness where before I saw only sin. I see loveliness and beauty that eludes me until I look at them in the light of the love of Jesus. My heart begins to soften, and my words are more inclined to follow in kind.

There is this, however: I never find it easy to think God's thoughts after Him, especially under duress. All hell conspires to make me forget what I know. "It is funny how mortals always picture us as putting things into their minds," C. S. Lewis's character Screwtape wrote to his demonic nephew. "In reality our best work is done in keeping things out."

We must, therefore, meditate on God's thoughts day and night to keep them on our minds. And we must pray as David Elginbrod prayed, "Grant that more an' more thoughts o' Thy thinking may come into our hearts day by day."

—Growing Slowly Wise

Malchus Comes to Mind

Again he asked them, "Who is it you want?"

And they said, "Jesus of Nazareth."

"I told you that I am he," Jesus answered. "If you are looking for me, then let these men go." This happened so that the words he had spoken would be fulfilled: "I have not lost one of those you gave me."

Then Simon Peter, who had a sword, drew it and struck the high priest's servant, cutting off his right ear. (The servant's name was Malchus.)

Jesus commanded Peter, "Put your sword away! Shall I not drink the cup the Father has given me?"

—John 18:7-11

I've often wondered why some non-Christians are so militantly anti-Christian, uncompromising and unreasonable in their hostility toward those of us who follow Jesus. Bashing believers seems to be their reason for being. It's an obsession that colors and controls all they think or say.

But the unbelievers who most touch my heart are those who've been wounded by well-meaning but witless believers who have hurt them with careless words or ways. Malchus comes to mind.

Malchus was in the band of soldiers who came to capture Jesus in the garden of Gethsemane—the one, in fact, whom Peter attacked. He was probably in the vanguard, showing particular zeal, for Peter would hardly have singled him out without reason. Peter took an awkward swing at his head and lopped off his ear, but Jesus at once stepped in, put an end to the conflict, calmed the crowd, and healed Malchus's bloody wound.

I've always wondered about Malchus. Did the two—he and Peter — know each other before this event in the garden? In those early days Peter was not an easy man to deal with. Had Peter, at some point, inflicted a much deeper wound, which Malchus would not let Jesus heal?

Later in the evening a servant related to Malchus lured Peter into his second denial (John 18:26–27), and I've often wondered (though I do not know) whether Malchus fingered the big fisherman. Perhaps Malchus took his hostility toward Jesus and His followers with him to the grave.

At a university where I used to serve, I recall a young atheist who fought with me on philosophical grounds for his unbelief—until in an unguarded moment he exposed the root of his resistance. When he was a child, he often thought about God and eagerly sought Him. One day a neighbor invited him to Sunday school, where the boy thought he'd surely meet his unknown God. Unfortunately his neighbor forgot that he had offered the invitation and left the boy sitting on his front curb, scrubbed and eagerly "waiting for Godot," who never showed up. The man did not call to apologize. Nor did he invite the boy again.

The boy's disappointment turned to bitterness toward a God who was disinclined to meet little boys, and so he turned his heart away. The young philosopher's antagonism came not from his head but from his heart. As Pascal observed a long time ago, the heart has reasons that reason doesn't have.

One proud lordly word, one needless contention . . . may blast the fruit of all you are doing.

—Richard Baxter

—*Out of the Ordinary*

Who's to Bless?

Then Melchizedek king of Salem brought out bread and wine. He
was priest of God Most High, and he blessed Abram, saying,
   "Blessed be Abram by God Most High,
   Creator of heaven and earth.
And blessed be God Most High,
   who delivered your enemies into your hand."
            —Genesis 14:18–20

Consider Abraham, returning from a raid on King Kedorlaomer and a coalition of Mesopotamian armies—battle scarred, exhausted, and fearful, well aware that he has angered four of the most powerful kings of his day. As he trudges through the valley of Shaveh, Melchizedek, the king of Salem, brings out bread and wine and *blesses* him.

"Without doubt the lesser person is blessed by the greater," said the writer of Hebrews (7:7), referring to this event. So who was this great high priest who blessed our great father Abraham?

Very little is known about Melchizedek—only that he was the king of Salem (ancient Jerusalem), that he was a "priest of God Most High," and that he fed and blessed the famished Abraham. Yet this king-priest has been lionized in the history of Israel and the church.

Commentators make much of Melchizedek's name, which means "King of Righteousness," but it was a common throne name in those days; the name is actually written in two parts, as though it were a title rather than a personal name.

The Essenes of Qumran thought Melchizedek was an angel. The philosopher Philo believed he was the divine *Logos.* The Jewish historian Josephus said he was only a man, but so righteous that he was "by common consent ... made a priest of God."

David saw Melchizedek as a prototype of the promised Messiah, who would establish a new order of king-priests (Psalm 110:1–4). The author of Hebrews, taking the argument further, said that Melchizedek was like Jesus, who is a priest despite His non-Levitical ancestry, whose title is "king of righteousness" and "king of peace," and who, because he appears in the account without beginning or end of life, "remains a priest *forever*" (Hebrews 7:2–3).

David and the writer of Hebrews have the last word, of course—Melchizedek is an Old Testament "type," or picture, of Jesus. But, as Josephus correctly noted, Melchizedek was also just a man and, as such, is an example of the kind of man I want to be.

I want to be a friend of souls. I want to stand by the side of the road, as Melchizedek did, waiting for weary travelers in the places, to quote Simon and Garfunkel, "where the ragged people go." I want to look for those who have been battered and wronged by others, who carry the dreary burden of a wounded and disillusioned heart. I want to nourish and refresh them with bread and wine and send them on their way with a benediction.

I cannot "fix" those who pass my way, though I may want to; but I can love them and listen to their hearts. I can pray with them. I can share a word of Scripture with them when it's appropriate. I can sing "sustaining songs," as lovers of Winnie the Pooh do. And I can leave them with a blessing.

A "blessing" is more than a parting shibboleth or a polite response to a sneeze. We bless others when we bring them to the One who is the source of all blessing. Melchizedek blessed Abram, saying, "Blessed be Abram *by God Most High.*" As Billy Graham would say, he blessed him *real good.*

To "bless" is to "bestow something that promotes or contributes to another's happiness, well-being, or prosperity." The Hebrew word comes from a root that means "to kneel," perhaps because of an ancient association between kneeling and receiving good from a benefactor.

In the Old Testament, God is the benefactor, the One who gives aid. He bestows the blessing. "This is how you are to bless the Israelites," God commanded Moses and Aaron:

> The Lord bless you
>   and keep you;
> the Lord make his face shine upon you

and be gracious to you;
the Lord turn his face toward you
and give you peace (Numbers 6:23–26).

I cannot strengthen feeble hands nor can I straighten knees that have given way, but I can bring weary travelers to the One who can. His bread offers endurance, strength, and eternal consolation. His wine gladdens and sustains the heart.

I cannot undo the cruel or dreary circumstances of anyone's journey nor can I take away their travail, but I can remind those who trudge by that there is One who walks with them—who holds them with His right hand, who guides them with His counsel, and afterward will take them into glory.

I cannot help the helpless, but I can love them, pray with them, and bring them to the throne of grace to find help in time of need. I cannot show them the way, but I can "show them God," as theologian John Piper says.

This is my blessing.

—*Out of the Ordinary*

The Tongue of a Learner

The Sovereign Lord has given me an instructed tongue,
to know the word that sustains the weary.
He wakens me morning by morning,
wakens my ear to listen like one being taught.
—Isaiah 50:4–5

Jesus said we shouldn't worry too much about what to say or how to say it. "At that time you will be given what to say" (Matthew 10:19). That's not to say that God fills our minds with thoughts we've never had before but rather that He takes from a reservoir of accumulated truth those things that He wants us to say. "Oration follows meditation," the old spiritual masters said.

Jesus said to His disciples, "What I tell you in the dark, speak in the daylight; what is whispered in your ear, proclaim from the roofs" (Matthew 10:27). These words are applicable to all of us. Our Lord speaks to us in solitude. There He tells us eternal and infinite secrets. There our eyes begin to see what only He can see; there our ears begin to detect the subtle undertones of His voice.

I listen to the Lord's word to Ezekiel: "Open your mouth and eat what I give you." Then Ezekiel looks and sees a hand stretched out to him, thrusting a scroll into his hand. Then the Lord says, "Son of man, eat what is before you, eat this scroll; then go and speak to the house of Israel." Ezekiel responds, "I opened my mouth, and he gave me the scroll to eat" (2:8–3:2).

Isaiah put it this way, speaking of the Servant of the Lord, the Messiah. What an intriguing image! Every morning God drew near His Servant, calling Him by name, awakening Him, inviting Him to sit at the Father's feet, giving Him His message for the day, preparing Him for each day's duties and demands. Every morning our Lord listened "like one being taught."

That's what enabled Jesus to speak such wise and gracious words to those in need. He knew the source of His wisdom. He said of Himself, "I . . . speak just what the Father has taught me"; I am "a man who has told you the truth that I heard from God"; "These words you hear are not my own; they belong to the Father" (John 8:28, 40; 14:24).

And so it is with us. Every morning our Lord invites us to sit at His feet, to listen like one being taught, to take what words we need for that day. That's how He gives us a wise, instructed tongue. That's how we "know the word that sustains the weary."

Some of the older translations render Isaiah 50:4: "The Lord God has given me the tongue of the *learned*." But the text actually speaks of "the tongue of a *learner*." We must be taught before we can teach others; we must learn before we can ever be "learned." And the more we receive, the more we have to give.

Ambrose, Augustine's mentor, wrote in the fourth century AD: "I desire . . . that, in the endeavor to teach, I may be able to learn. For one is the true Master, who alone has not learnt, what He taught all; but men learn before they teach, and receive from Him what they may hand on to others."

It's through prayerful, thoughtful Bible reading and quiet meditation that our Lord speaks from His depths to ours. It is when we give ourselves time for prayerful contemplation that His heart is revealed and our hearts are exposed. We must listen until we know what He feels, what He wants, what He loves, and what He hates. Then we can give that word away.

"Hide yourself in God," George MacDonald said, "and when you rise before men, speak out of that secret place." When we speak out of the secret place, we have the overwhelming authority of God. We are saying again what God has said—nothing more and nothing less.

In our relativistic and subjectivist world, the notion of a decisive and final word from God sounds presumptuous. Discovery, dialogue, and debate are more in vogue. But we must never forget that God's word is exactly that—God's word. Behind every word we speak lies the infinite power and authority of God Himself, an authority mediated through every utterance. Thus Peter wrote, "If anyone speaks, he should do it *as one speaking the very words of God*" (1 Peter 4:11).

—Out of the Ordinary

The Manner and Message

The Lord's servant must not quarrel; instead, he must be kind to everyone, able to teach, not resentful.
—2 Timothy 2:24

Christians never seem to fit in. As early as the second century AD, they had to defend themselves against charges of atheism because they failed to defer to the gods, of incest because they talked about loving their brothers and sisters, of cannibalism because they gathered to "eat" the body of Christ, of being antisocial because they didn't participate in the games, and of being anti-intellectual because in contrast to Plato and his disciples they believed that truth was found in the particulars and not in the universals alone.

Then, as now, Christians found penetrating society difficult. But penetration is the name of the game. Without it, we're good for nothing, like salt that has lost its tang. We've got to mingle more; we've got to gain a greater measure of solidarity with the world and win the right to be heard. Jesus did; He socialized with the irreligious. We tend to cluster too much, to enjoy one another's company at the expense of those outside. Unfortunately, we've not learned from our Lord the principle He taught and exemplified so well. There is no lasting influence without sustained and loving contact.

Our standoffish techniques reflect that lack of solid contact. The gospel through bumper stickers, T-shirts, billboards, and lapel buttons may earn us derision but not a hearing. They don't communicate; they alienate. Furthermore, we ought to resist Madison Avenue's invasion of our realm. Witnessing has to do with loving relationships, not sales technique. Thinking in terms of a broad smile and getting one's patter down pat only mechanizes and trivializes the gospel. As John Naisbitt pointed out, the world has gone cold; it needs to be "repersonalized." Most people are looking for someone who cares.

We've got to get natural and down to earth. Tertullian, an early Roman Christian, described witnesses this way: "We [Christians] live among you [non-Christians], eat the same food, wear the same clothes, have the same habits and the same necessities of existence. We are not gymnosophists [a kooky sect encountered in India by Alexander the Great] who dwell in the woods and exile ourselves from ordinary human life . . . We sojourn with you in the world renouncing neither forum, nor market, nor bath, nor booth, nor workshop, nor inn . . . We sail with you, we fight with you, we till the ground with you, we join with you in business ventures."

Christianity can be lived in a real world of people and things. It has to be lived there to be lived at all. It was meant for the marketplace. We've also got to find proper ways to talk to our modern friends about God. Traditional words are almost defunct. The problem is familiarity. Most non-Christians have heard the words. They're familiar with the lingo. We need innovative and novel proclamation. Of course, there's nothing novel about the gospel itself. The Good News isn't avant-garde. We don't go on, we go back—back to Christ and the apostles for our message. But the old message can't be delivered in the same old way.

The language and style of the New Testament in general was not that of classical Greek literature but the language of the common people, the bold, idiomatic street talk of the day. There were no special holy words. Plain speech to common people has always been God's way.

And finally we must manifest the kindly spirit of the apostle when he wrote: "And the Lord's servant must not quarrel; instead, he must be kind to everyone, able to teach, not resentful. Those who oppose him he must gently instruct, in the hope that God will grant them repentance leading them to a knowledge of the truth, and that they will come to their senses and escape from the trap of the devil, who has taken them captive to do his will" (2 Timothy 2:24–26).

There's no need to do fierce battle with non-Christians, no reason to pin them wriggling against the wall. It is, in fact, a sin to be quarrelsome and argumentative. Although we may have to enter into controversy, as our Lord did, woe to the man who enjoys it. Unfortunately some of us are always spoiling for a fight and are like the man who stopped to watch a street fight and inquired, "Is this a private fight or can anyone join in?"

Sad to say, the fighting is sometimes dirty—name calling and verbal abuse.

Discussion and debate on the facts is one thing; personal attack and insult is another. When we resort to innuendo and verbal grenades, we've already lost our moral and rational force.

And so we must avoid what Paul called "foolish and stupid arguments" (2 Timothy 2:23). Rather, we must be courteous in our demeanor ("kind to everyone"), intelligent and relevant in our declaration of truth ("able to teach"), and nondefensive in our posture ("not resentful"). Let us gently instruct those who oppose us "in the hope that God will grant them repentance leading them to a knowledge of the truth, and that they will come to their senses and escape from the trap of the devil, who has taken them captive to do his will" (2:24–26).

Those who oppose are not the enemy; they are the victims of the enemy, duped by him to do his will. Satan has captivated them, but truth linked with love may deliver them.

Manner and message are inextricably linked; one necessarily goes with the other. Truth alone is not enough. Without grace truth is mere dogma and in the end hardens and brutalizes. And of course love can never stand alone. Without truth it becomes mere sentimentalism. Thus there are two liberating elements: truth and love. Only truth delivered with courtesy has power to change an opponent's mind. Apparently the Good News sounds good only when announced with good manners.

—*The Strength of a Man*

Playing God and Other Perils

Brothers, do not slander one another. Anyone who speaks against
his brother or judges him speaks against the law and judges it.
When you judge the law, you are not keeping it, but sitting in
judgment on it. There is only one Lawgiver and Judge, the one
who is able to save and destroy. But you—
who are you to judge your neighbor?
—James 4:11–12

The etymology of James's word *slander* suggests "speaking *down*." Linked with his other word, *judging*, it implies an inclination to put a brother down. Paul makes a similar observation, "Why do you judge your brother? Or why do you *look down* on your brother?" (Romans 14:10).

Certainly it's unacceptable to tolerate wrong actions or condone an environment that allows wrong actions to occur. In the midst of our culture's addled and confused notion of tolerance—a tolerance that says we cannot critique anyone's idea of right and wrong—we must affirm the necessity of knowing what one should and should not do. God has given His word and calls on us to discern between good and evil; good judgment is a mark of maturity. As G. K. Chesterton pointed out, "Morality, like art, consists of drawing a straight line."

Some have made Jesus' words, "Judge not, that you be not judged" (Matthew 7:1 NKJV) an admonition to turn a blind eye to others' faults, but that can't be what He meant when in the same breath He says that we should not "give dogs what is sacred" or "throw pearls to pigs" (Matthew 7:6). That caution assumes that we can and must recognize cynical and profane people when we see them. In the same way, Jesus admonished His disciples to "judge for yourselves what is right" (Luke 12:57).

Jesus' and James's injunctions against judging are not about drawing straight lines but about condemning others and writing them off—judging them without mercy and without caring for their souls. Put another way, judging, in the sense James employs the word, is a matter of being *merely just.*

It's good that God is not merely just. If He were, we would be in a world of trouble, for He would judge every one of us at this moment. He would cut down cruel and monstrous tyrants everywhere, true, but He would also put down our cruelty and petty tyranny. "Are not the gods just?" C. S. Lewis's Psyche asked her wise mentor in the novel *Till We Have Faces.* "Oh, no, my child," was the reply. "Where would we be if they were?"

I recall a conversation between Robinson Crusoe and his Man Friday: "Well," said Friday, "you say God is so strong, so great; has he not as much strong, as much might as the devil?"

"Yes, yes, Friday," Crusoe replied, "God is much stronger than the devil."

"But if God much strong, much might as the devil, why God no kill the devil so make him no more do wicked?"

"You might as well ask," Crusoe answered reflectively, "Why does God not kill you and me when we do wicked things that offend?"

The point is that God has every right to kill you and me instantly the moment we do any wicked thing, but He has chosen to show compassion. God will judge the world in due time, but for now He is reserving final judgment. Would that you and I were more like our Father.

I know the world in which I live, a world of my own, the narrow world of my mind—haughty, unforgiving, and judgmental. How readily I pronounce judgment on others' motives and behavior though I have neither the knowledge nor the authority to do so.

Judging others doesn't seem like much of a sin, but James would have us believe it's a serious breach of the Law of Love (James 2:8). When I condemn my brother, I'm not a lover but a judge—a judge of my own brother and of my Father's law, interpreting it and modifying it to mean what I think it ought to mean—rescinding it on occasion. Better that I love my brother as he is and let God deal with his imperfections. That's "sloppy *agape,*" you say. I say I'd rather love too many than too few.

Furthermore, when I condemn my brother, I'm playing God—infringing on His rights as the judge of all the earth. "There is only one Lawgiver and

Judge, the one who is able to save and destroy," says James. Then his bony finger rises out of the text and points directly at me: "But you [Yes, I'm talking to you!]— who are you to judge your neighbor?" (James 4:12).

Some actions are easy to identify as sin, but judging is much more elusive. It's hard to know the difference between discernment and ungodly condemnation. Where exactly is the line? I don't always know, and even when I do I don't always get it right, but here are some thoughts that have helped me.

There's a firm maxim that all proper judgment of my brother begins with *self*-judgment. I cannot discern another's sin until I sit in judgment on my own. "How can you say to your brother, 'Let me take the speck out of your eye,' when all the time there is a plank in your own eye?" (Matthew 7:4). When confronted with a brother's offenses, the humble heart turns first to itself and to God.

Further, I must not go "beyond what is written" (1 Corinthians 4:6) and make binding for others what Scripture does not bind. It's possible for me to judge a brother not because he's unlike Jesus but because he's unlike me. I need to know that others can be strange, offbeat, eccentric, unusual, and marching to a different drummer without being sinful and morally out of step. "Who are you to judge someone else's servant?" Paul says of my private scruples. "To his own master he stands or falls. And he will stand, for the Lord is able to make him stand" (Romans 14:4). Where Scripture is silent, I must be silent.

Finally, I must not judge another's motives. I've never seen a motive and wouldn't know one if I saw it. I must never say, "You did this because . . ." Heart-motives are beyond my ken.

Scripture is full of examples of mistaken assumptions, like those of Job's friends who were convinced his suffering was the result of profound sin. Yet they were wrong. Only God saw the whole picture. With the limited insight we have, a faulty verdict is assured.

It's good to ask those who seem to have gone wrong, "Can you tell me why you did what you did?" We may be surprised at what we learn. Even if we can't fully understand another's intentions, it will help us become more understanding.

> The purposes of a man's heart are deep waters,
>> but a man of understanding draws them out (Proverbs 20:5).

It's an old saying: "Know another's burden, and then you won't be able to speak except in pity."

Years ago I heard a true story that illustrates this insight. It seems a young salesman worked for a company whose president gave turkeys to all his employees at Christmas. The man was a bachelor, didn't know how to roast a turkey, and didn't particularly want to learn. Every year he had to figure out how to rid himself of the thing.

On the day the turkeys were handed out, a couple of the man's friends purloined the bird tagged with his name and substituted a dummy made of papier mâché. The bogus bird was then presented with due formality, and our man, with turkey tucked under his arm, caught his bus for home.

As it happened, he seated himself next to a man whose melancholy was obvious. Feeling compassion for him, the salesman began a conversation that revealed the other man's bitter circumstances: He had lost his job and had almost no money for Christmas—only a couple of dollars with which to purchase a few groceries for Christmas dinner. His funds were insufficient for anything but bare essentials.

The man with the turkey sized up the situation and realized he had the solution to both of their problems. He could unload the turkey in a way that was mutually beneficial. His first thought was to give it away; his second was to sell it for the few dollars, thinking that his new friend could salvage his dignity by paying for the meal.

And so he proposed the sale, explaining his dilemma and his resolution of it. The other man was elated, the exchange was made, and the bird was taken home to wife and kiddies, who presumably gathered excitedly around the table while the turkey was unwrapped, only to discover that the bird their father had bought was a fraud.

You can imagine the disappointment and indignation of the defrauded family. The well-meaning turkey vendor, however, went home satisfied that he had done a good deed for the day. I'm told that when he returned to work after the holidays and learned what his associates had done, he devoted most of his free time for the next month trying to track down the victim of his unintended scam, but he never saw the man again.

The offended family must believe that they were the victims of a cruel hoax—a classic example of man's inhumanity to man—but they would be wrong. The man's intentions were wholly good.

"Judge nothing before the appointed time," warned Paul. "Wait till the Lord comes. He will bring to light what is hidden in darkness and will expose the motives of men's hearts. At that time each will receive his praise from God" (1 Corinthians 4:5–6).

Judgment is presumptuous on my part; only God knows the heart. And it's premature—I must wait until Jesus comes. Time and God will give final judgment. Until then I must wait.

—*Growing Slowly Wise*

God Will Judge Evil

But they will have to give account to him who is ready to judge
the living and the dead.
—1 Peter 4:5

We see thugs, tyrants, and other terrible women and men getting away with appalling evil around the world.

We read the newspaper and shake our heads over depravity's inexorable advance through our culture, within our government, and through our educational systems.

Sometimes we wonder if God is minding the store.

Why doesn't He do something?

We ask the question because we see only one side of God—His mercy and long-suffering patience. But God's tolerance is not the whole story. He is wonderfully gracious, incredibly patient, and not willing that any should perish. But if a man or a woman continues to spurn His grace and patience, if he or she will not listen, will not relent, will not turn—there is nothing left but death—and after death the judgment (1 Peter 4:5).

Though it may seem to us at times that the wicked make their way through the world unscathed by their evil, there is a forgotten factor in the equation. That factor is death, the great equalizer. Death stalks men and women relentlessly. "The statistics are very impressive," George Bernard Shaw grumbled. "One out of every one person dies." There's no escape for anyone once born. "Man is destined to die . . . and after that to face judgment" (Hebrews 9:27). "Payday someday!" Robert G. Lee, a preacher of another era said.

A few years ago I stood in the mummy chamber of the Egyptian Museum and looked down at the shrunken remains of Ramses the Great and said to myself, *Is this the man who terrorized the ancient Near Eastern world?*

Jean Massilon, the French bishop of Clermont, put it well when he looked down on the heads of state of all Europe, gathered in the Cathedral of Notre Dame for the funeral of Louis XIV (who called himself Louis the Great). "Brethren," said the bishop, "in the hour of death, no one is great." Nothing settles the score quite like death.

In Psalm 73 one of Israel's poets struggled with the issue of the evil that people do that is not requited in their lifetimes. They "have no struggles," he grumbled. The godless scoff at God, persecute his people, and get away with murder, the poet complained. "Surely in vain have I kept my heart pure" (73:13).

But then the psalmist recalled the fact of death and destruction:

> Surely you place them on slippery ground;
>   you cast them down to ruin.
> How suddenly are they destroyed,
>   completely swept away by terrors!
> As a dream when one awakes,
>   so when you arise, O Lord,
> you will despise them as fantasies (73:18–20).

The ungodly are on a slippery slope to the grave; they are cast down to ruin, they are destroyed, they are completely swept away by terrors!

The Hebrew word for *terrors* is a poetic designation for the abode of the dead—a place of speechless desolation and destruction. There, as Lewis said, they "will be left utterly and absolutely outside, repelled, exiled, estranged, finally and unspeakably ignored!"

"Do not be deceived," Paul wrote, "God cannot be mocked. A man reaps what he sows. The one who sows to please his sinful nature, from that nature will reap destruction" (Galatians 6:7).

Paul wrote again to those who have thumbed their noses at God:

> Do you think you will escape God's judgment? Or do you show contempt for the riches of his kindness, tolerance and patience, not realizing that God's kindness leads you toward repentance?
>
> But because of your stubbornness and your unrepentant heart, you are storing up wrath against yourself for the day of God's wrath,

when his righteous judgment will be revealed. God "will give to each person according to what he has done" (Romans 2:3–6).

God yearns over sinful men and women with unutterable sorrow. "There is not one waif of humanity excluded from the warm zone of His infinite compassion and tender pity," wrote F. B. Meyer. God's love lingers over every lost soul.

"How can I give you up, Ephraim?" God said of Israel through His tears.

> How can I hand you over, Israel?
> How can I treat you like Admah?
>   How can I make you like Zeboiim?
> My heart is changed within me;
>   all my compassion is aroused (Hosea 11:8).

There is no one that God will not save, *but there is no one He will save against his or her will.* His patience endures as long as there is the slightest hope of repentance, but if people do not want God's love, then He will not foist it on them. In that sense, hell, though it seems odd to say it, may be just another provision of God's love. He loves us enough to leave us alone.

But understand what that means—eternal life without law, without love, without laughter, without beauty, without any of the elements that make life worthwhile. God is the giver of every good and perfect gift and the source of everything that is good and true and beautiful. His absence means the absence of everything that gives meaning to existence. If that's what hell is, then Lewis was right: Hell is exactly the right name for what it would be.

I'm reminded of the day our Lord was passing through Samaria on His way to Jerusalem. He sent messengers ahead to prepare a place, but the people of Samaria rejected Him.

When James and John heard about the refusal, they fumed, "Lord, do you want us to call fire down from heaven to destroy them?" (Luke 9:54). They had been on the Mount of Transfiguration and had seen their Lord with Moses and Elijah. Elijah and his fiery judgment were fresh in their minds. But when they asked for similar judgment, Jesus turned and rebuked them.

Later manuscripts add an explanatory statement, supplying the content of the rebuke: "You do not know what kind of spirit you are of, for the Son of Man did not come to destroy men's lives, but to save them."

Whether the addition is a scribal emendation or belongs to the text, I leave to scholars to decide. I do think, however, that it accurately reflects Jesus' thoughts. It is not our business to judge God's enemies. He treads out the winepress of His wrath alone (see Isaiah 63:3). Our business is to bring salvation to the world.

"Be merciful to those who doubt," Jude wrote, "snatch others from the fire and save them; to others show mercy, mixed with fear—hating even the clothing stained by corrupted flesh" (Jude 22–23).

Some unbelievers are close to salvation but still unconvinced. Persuade them.

Others are close to destruction. Snatch them from the fire and save them if you can.

Still others—the saddest of all—have hardened their hearts against the truth and will not be influenced. Have mercy on them mixed with fear: There but for the grace of God go you and I.

Despise the garments contaminated by sin, but don't despise the sinners! Show them compassion and love them to the end. They are not our enemies; they're tragic victims of a terrible, merciless enemy, taken captive by him to do his will (see 2 Timothy 2:26).

But "if love will not compel them to come in, we must leave them to God, the judge of all," John Wesley said. "Will not the Judge of all the earth do right?" (Genesis 18:25).

It's that assurance that keeps us steady in the face of all the evil that men and women do. It's that unshakable truth to which we may cling as the Enemy's shadow falls over our nation and culture. We can take evil seriously, but we needn't panic in the face of its steady advance. Why? Because we know that God's processes are perfectly adequate to deal with the worst that perverse and villainous people can do. That confidence results in poise in the face of appalling, disorienting disorder. The oft-quoted motto to the contrary, you *can* keep your head when all others are losing theirs, because you *do* understand the situation.

Saint John of the Cross said that those who know God and what He is doing have three distinguishing characteristics—tranquillity, gentleness, and strength. That suggests to me an immense depth, an invulnerable steadiness, and an ability to respond with kindness and care for others out of a center of quiet rest.

Frenzy, fury, hysteria, intensity, impatience, instability, pessimism, and every other kind of fuss and ferocity are marks of an immature soul. Those who know that "God works in tranquillity," as one saint put it, share the calm and quiet nature of the One "who works out everything in conformity with the purpose of his will" (Ephesians 1:11).

—Elijah

Finishing Well

Go and tell Hezekiah, "This is what the Lord, the God of your
father David, says: I have heard your prayer and seen your tears;
I will add fifteen years to your life."
—Isaiah 38:5

King Hezekiah ruled well for fourteen years.

He removed the high places, smashed the sacred stones, and cut down
the Asherah poles. He broke into pieces the bronze snake Moses had
made, for up to that time the Israelites had been burning incense to
it. (It was called Nehushtan.) Hezekiah trusted in the Lord, the God
of Israel. There was no one like him among all the kings of Judah,
either before him or after him. He held fast to the Lord and did not
cease to follow him; he kept the commands the Lord had given Moses
(2 Kings 18:4–6).

But Hezekiah, I'm sad to say, frittered the last years of his life away.

The turning point was Hezekiah's illness, during which the prophet Isaiah
came to him with a word from the Lord: "Put your house in order," he said,
"because you are going to die" (Isaiah 38:1). Hezekiah had been working on
the tapestry of his life, "rolling it up like a weaver," to use his vivid metaphor (Isaiah 38:12). Now the roll had grown large enough—his work was
finished—and God was about to cut the cloth from the loom.

The king argued strenuously and tearfully that he could serve God better
by living, in answer to which, for some inscrutable reason, the Lord relented

and added fifteen years to his life. Unfortunately Hezekiah did not make the most of his additional years.

When the son of the king of mighty Babylon came with his glittering entourage to pay respects to tiny Judah, Hezekiah, flushed with a sense of his own importance, showed off "his" national treasury while the Babylonians looked on politely, making a mental note to loot it. "I showed them *everything*," Hezekiah boasted to Isaiah. The prophet's response was to inform the king that "everything" was exactly what the Babylonians would seize (39:3–7).

Assured that Judah's doom lay well in the future, however, Hezekiah comforted himself with the self-centered conceit that at least there'd be ease and affluence in his days. He could kick back and indulge himself in careless retirement, which, I believe, is the reason for the foolishness of his final years. For the truth is, we can't just kick back, marking time: We're either growing toward God, or we're going in the other direction.

There's nothing wrong with retiring and setting a slower pace for oneself, but retirement is not the chief end of man. We must grow, mature, serve, minister, mentor, and venture ourselves to the end of our days.

You may have heard of John Steven Akhwari, the runner from Tanzania who finished last in the marathon at the 1968 Olympics in Mexico City. No last-place finisher in a marathon ever finished quite so last.

Injured along the way, he hobbled into the stadium over an hour after the last runner had crossed the finish line. All the spectators were gone, the stadium was closed, and crews were preparing for the closing ceremony when Akhwari gathered himself for a final effort and *sprinted* across the line. (I'm told that one of the workers picked up a torn finishing tape and held it across the track so Akhwari could break it.)

When Bud Greenspan, the official filmmaker of the games, asked the weary athlete why he put himself through such pain, Akhwari replied, "Mr. Greenspan, my country did not send me five thousand miles to start the race. They sent me to *finish* it."

To idle away our last years in self-indulgence and indolence is to rob others and ourselves of the best that is yet to be. Even when "old and gray," we can declare God's

> power to the next generation,
> [His] might to all who are to come (Psalm 71:18).

There is yet service to be rendered and victories to be won. "Give your fruit before it rots," Richard Rolle said. Finish strong!

—Out of the Ordinary

Forever Home

I will dwell in the house of the Lord forever.
—Psalm 23:6

There's a natural watershed in our lives. We reach the top, stand for a moment, and then we're over the hill. Everything is downhill from that moment on. But no matter; we're headed for home.

Home—that's where my heart is.

"I have come home at last!" shouted C. S. Lewis's heaven-struck unicorn as he stamped his right forefoot on the ground. "I have come here at last! This is my real country! I belong here. This is the land I have been looking for all my life, though I never knew it until now. The reason why we loved the old Narnia is that it sometimes looked a little like this."

It's not that heaven is somewhat like home. It *is* home. Our earthly homes are mere signs or reflections—primitive symbols of warmth, love, together-ness, and familiarity. The ultimate reality is our Father's house—where there is a father who never dies, who makes a home for the lonely, who treats us like family; where real love awaits us; where we're included—"taken in."

We hear about Odysseus, the Flying Dutchman, Frodo, and E.T., and we too want to go home—to that place where everything is impervious to change, where God will wipe every tear from our eyes, where everyone has a friend, where love will never end, where everything finally works out for good.

Everything goes wrong here; nothing will go wrong there. Nothing will be lost; nothing will be missing; nothing will fall apart or go down the drain. Heaven is God's answer to Murphy's Law.

Not all our hurts can be healed in this life. There are wounds we will bear all our lives, but, as a friend once said to me, "If you hold your wounds up to the sunlight of God's love, they will never fester and in heaven they will be healed." Some harm awaits heaven's cure. That's where, as C. S. Lewis said, that "great bleeding wound from which all of us suffer will be eternally healed."

In this life we're delivered from shame, guilt, and fear by God's forgiving love; there is substantial improvement, but there's no complete healing. We were born with broken hearts, and some sense of that brokenness will be with us throughout our days on earth. We'll never quite be whole. There will always be some measure of inner pain that will co-exist with our joy and peace, some vague longing—"homesickness"—that will linger until we get home. We are satisfied here but never quite content.

One of these days we'll go home, and then everything will be complete. Think of a place where there is no sin, no sorrow, no quarrels, no threats, no abandonment, no insecurity, no struggling with sagging self-worth. Heaven is where everything that makes us sad will be banished. We will be delivered from everything that has defiled or disrupted our lives.

It's disturbing to look ahead and see the same impossible road stretching out in front of us, going on indefinitely. We're driven to despair or rebellion when we think there's no point to our misery and no end to it. That's why we find comfort in the realization that it will *not* go on forever. One day everything that God has been doing will be done. He will come for us, and we will go home.

It may surprise you to know that David knew that much about heaven. Most folks who read the Old Testament never think to look for heaven there, but it occurs—in symbol and song, in metaphor and type. Ancient people took to analogy much better than we. They drew pictures: green pastures, Elysian Fields, light. One of the most convincing images is that of God Himself "taking us in."

The thought occurs in the story of Enoch, who walked with God for three hundred years, and "then he was no more, because God took him away" (Genesis 5:24). Enoch and God took a walk one day and got too far from home. The old patriarch was too weary to walk all the way back, so God took him.

One of Israel's singers saw himself and others as "destined for the grave," but as he goes on to say,

God will redeem my life from the grave;
> *he will surely take me to himself* (Psalm 49:15).

And then there's the poet who learned God's presence from his peril: "I am always with you," he concluded. For now,

you hold me by my right hand.
You guide me with your counsel,
> and afterward you will take me into glory (Psalm 73:23–26).

Taken in. I like that way of looking at my death. It reminds me of something Jesus said: "I am going there to prepare a place for you. And if I go and prepare a place for you, I will come back and *take* you to be with me that you also may be where I am" (John 14:2–3).

That's the fundamental revelation of heaven in both Testaments: being taken in, welcomed, received, embraced, and included. Death for God's children is not bitter frustration but mere transition into a larger and permanent love—a love undisturbed by time, unmenaced by evil, unbroken by fear, unclouded by doubt.

All God's idylls end favorably; all God's children "live happily forever after." That's the most cherished article of my creed.

Never again will they hunger;
> never again will they thirst.
The sun will not beat upon them,
> nor any scorching heat.
For the Lamb at the center of the throne will be their shepherd;
> he will lead them to springs of living water.
And God will wipe away every tear from their eyes (Revelation 7:16–17).
> *—Psalm 23*

Note to the Reader

The publisher invites you to share your response to the message of this book by writing Discovery House Publishers, P.O. Box 3566, Grand Rapids, MI 49501, U.S.A. For information about other Discovery House books, music, videos, or DVDs, contact us at the same address or call 1-800-653-8333. Find us on the Internet at http://www.dhp.org/ or send e-mail to books@dhp.org.

About the Author

Davld Roper and his wife, Carolyn, offer encouragement and counsel to pastoral couples through Idaho Mountain Ministries. David served on the pastoral staff of Peninsula Bible Church in Palo Alto, California, and as senior pastor of Cole Community Church in Boise, Idaho. His many books include *Psalm 23: The Song of a Passionate Heart* and *In Quietness and Confidence*.

FAITH is being sure of what we do NoT see.
Heb 11v1

FAITH CAN NOT Be generAted, It is A gift
of God given iN ANswer To prayer,
Do you WANT To see God iN His GloRy?
PrAy ThAT The eyes of your hearTs mAy
Be eNLighTeNed ThAT you mAy see...
                                    Eph 1v18

Pg 79|

FAITH grows As we feed oN God's woRd
"FAITH comes by hearing The messAge,
And The messAge is heard ~~by~~ Through
The woRd of ChrisT. Rom 10v17

ABRAhams ANswer To IsAAc "God will
Provide" This is The ANswer To every
oNe of Lifes dilemmAs,
ABRAHAm CAlled The mouNTAiN
MORIAH meaNiNg "God will provide"

LAMININ
2 chron 20   -JehoshaphAt
"We do NoT KNow whAT To Do, buT
our eyes ARe upoN You.
                2 Chron 20 v10-12